LESSONS THAT RHYME ...STAY IN THE MIND

A REFRESHING NEW WAY TO LEARN THE GOLF SWING.

CHARLES SORRELL

PGA MASTER PROFESSIONAL

with Paul deVere

Saron Press, Ltd.
Hilton Head Island, South Carolina

Lessons That Rhyme...Stay In The Mind:
A refreshing new way to learn the golf swing

 SARON PRESS, LTD.
Box 4990
Hilton Head Island, South Carolina 29938
http://members.aol.com/saronpress
e-mail: saron@digitel.net
VOICE: (803) 363-6697 / FAX: (803) 363-6698

Copyright © 1996 by Charles Sorrell and Paul deVere
Edited, Layout, Cover Design by Lewis Hammet
Illustrated by Shuichi Kuga / Graphics Support by Michael Reinsch
Design, Inc. / Additional Graphics by Richard W. Flemming of N&R
Printing. Printed in the United States of America by N&R Printing.
All rights reserved.

Library of Congress Catalog Card Number: 96-092885
ISBN: 0-9650791-2-0

For ordering information please
contact the publisher. Quantity discounts.

To My Wife...

When you enter beautiful Golf Meadows, you come to a small pond on your right. It even has a name: Lake Joyce. The marker there reads, "Just as this water is a necessary ingredient to the success of Golf Meadows, she is the one ingredient that is vital to all phases of my life."

For your love, dedication and support of me and all my efforts, I dedicate this book and my life to you, Joyce Barr Sorrell.

Table of Contents

Lessons That Rhyme...Stay In The Mind

Acknowledgments

To my Creator for giving me the talent to play the game at its highest level and to share what I have learned with students the world over. To the PGA of America for allowing me to become part of that great organization. To the thousands of students whom I have had the privilege of teaching; one of my greatest joys is to see you reach your personal goals. To all those who had faith in me and my efforts to complete this book, and for helping me see it through. To the many friends I have met all over this great country who've sat and listened to what I had to say about the golf swing. And finally, to the game itself, for the magnetism it has, the challenge it holds and the opportunities it has afforded me. I am forever grateful. Thank you.

Preface

On Rhyme and Reason

In 1990, when I had the extraordinary experience of being named Teacher of the Year by the PGA of America, I was overwhelmed. This significant honor allowed me to develop a relationship, through letters, with a fellow teacher for whom I have unlimited respect. He was Teacher of the Year in 1989, and his name was Harvey Penick.

We became what you might call 'pen pals,' and I often wrote him with questions I had about teaching the golf swing. The letters we exchanged I will treasure all my life. In one particularly poignant note, Mr. Penick summed up quite eloquently my feelings on the art of teaching golf:

> Dear Charles:
> . . . You asked in your letter if I did not think that the game of golf could be enjoyed by so many more people if we teachers simply aimed the player, straightened his grip and let things happen. *That is all I have ever done with most everyone.*
> — *Harvey Penick*

This book is meant to simplify the golf swing. I remain in Mr. Penick's shadow.

All my teaching life I've attempted to make the game I love approachable to anyone who wanted to learn how to play it. And I've come to appreciate that I've learned more from my students than I could ever teach them.

Golfers are an interesting lot. They don't just bring hooks and slices to the lesson tee; they bring themselves. That's what has made my career as a teacher so rewarding. Whether they're doctors or truck drivers, lawyers or homemakers, every one of them can slice a ball equally well. No matter who they have observed or what they do, they still have problems getting off their right foot when they swing the club. (*Note to lefthanders*: Please excuse my right-handed references. Where possible, I've tried to make these instructions fit your situation as well. In fact, I actually like to teach lefthanders because we can look at each other when we swing. You've also forced me to keep improving my left-handed swing, and for this righthander, that's been tough.)

Here's another thing I've learned about golfers in general: They grow weary and glassy-eyed when I slip up and start using words like "swing plane" and "weight transfer" without properly defining them first. I think one of the major problems in learning the golf swing is the continual frustration students face when trying to wade through terms that, while they might make sense to teachers and some golf junkies, are a foreign language to most.

Several years ago, one of my students from a ladies' clinic came up to me and told me, with a straight face, "Charlie, I don't know if my cupped wrist is inside or out."

We went inside and had a lemonade.

Of course, some golf jargon is unavoidable. A few words and phrases actually do make sense. But in the following chapters, I've done my best to either avoid jargon altogether or fully explain it as I go.

In fact, it was all that jargon that got me started on rhyming. That and the glassy eyes. Students of the game spent an enormous amount of time and money attempting to bring what they learned from the lesson tee to the golf course. As I watched them walk up to the spot where it all begins on hole No. 1, I saw the confidence and new-found knowledge slough off them like a snake shedding its skin. I don't think it had anything to do with the correctness of what I had taught them. I think it had to do with human nature. Down deep, we're all "old dogs," and it's tough learning new tricks — like a better, more consistent golf swing. Without a friendly reminder now and again, we all have a tendency to revert to our old ways.

Lessons That Rhyme ...

Golf is a game — it's supposed to be fun. All my technical talk about "spine angles" wasn't tickling anybody's funny bone. There had to be a better way . . . and there was.

Rhymes. We learned them as kids. They've carried us through the good times and the bad. Remembering rhymes is easy, pleasant and fun. You can take them to the tee and use them as a mental cue. They don't get in the way. Actually, I've found they can help you with your entire game.

My rhymes aren't Shakespeare (my college English professor would blush if he saw some of these). But based on the often dramatic improvements I've seen in my students, they sure seem to work.

In *Lessons That Rhyme . . . Stay In The Mind*, I'll make you three promises:

(1) I'll try to avoid golf jargon, or at least explain it clearly if I have to use a little;

(2) I'll give you rhymes that will dramatically improve your game; and

(3) I'll bring a smile back to your face as you play the game of a lifetime!

Introduction

"Charlie Jargon"

Before we get started, I'd like to go ahead and introduce you to some of the terms I'll be using throughout the book. This is "Charlie jargon." My desire is that it will be clear and easy to understand. You may have heard these terms by different names, but I like to keep things simple. Sometimes golf instruction sounds like rocket-science gibberish. Well, let's leave the scientific stuff to NASA.

On the Swing

In this book, I've concentrated on the full swing. You'll be reading (and seeing) the golf swing broken up into different areas. I use a little different terminology than maybe you're used to. So let's be good scouts and get prepared.

1. *The Address Position* is the arrangement of body parts as they assume a ready position just before the swing motion begins. That's simple enough.

2. *Swing-A-Way* is the first half of the Backswing movement. It begins the moment you swing the club away from the ball. It ends as the club shaft reaches a location that is horizontal to the ground and positioned vertically above the *toe line*.

Yes, *toe line* is right out of the golf jargon books, but it's one of the few terms that's not too mysterious.

After assuming the Address Position, the swing motion is made up of four basic movements — the Backswing, Downswing, Forwardswing and Up-and-Around-Swing. To see these broken down even further. Refer to pages 4 - 5 in Chapter 1.

Everything in golf is based upon the "target line" — the imaginary line between two very real points: where your ball is . . . and where your target is located.

Draw an imaginary, straight line that will touch the tip of both your toes when they are at a right angle and parallel to the *target line.* There's another one. *Target line.* But that's not too bad either. Put yourself on a par 3 hole. Draw another imaginary straight line from the hole, your target, through the ball. That's the *target line.* You've got to be six or seven steps behind the ball and looking toward the target to effectively determine this line.

By the way, *everything in golf is based on this line!*

Some folks tell you to imagine two railroad tracks. The one your standing on is the *toe line.* The one the ball is on is the *target line.* If that works for you, fine.

But I like to think of those two lines as an interstate highway cutting across some flat Texas landscape. All you can see are those two lines of asphalt coming and going for miles and miles. For me, the *toe line/target line* is a Texas interstate. Anyway, it's been years since I rode a train.

3. *Backswing* is the completed movement of the club and body after the Swing-A-Way has been completed, with body and club in a position ready to begin the downswing.

4. *Downswing* is when the hands are moving downward and the body has responded properly. The hands have not quite reached hip level at the end of the Downswing movement.

5. *Forwardswing* is when the hands begin to move forward, assisted by other bodily movements, after the Downswing movement has been completed.

6. *Impact* is were the club collides with the ball.

7. *End of Forwardswing* is when both arms are fully extended — forming the "arms" of a "Y" — while the club shaft forms the tail of the "Y." This happens after Impact has occurred and the clubhead is approximately two feet past where the ball was located.

Lessons That Rhyme ...

8. *Up-and-Around-Swing* refers to both your body and the clubhead; the clubhead is traveling upward while the body is rotating in a more circular motion until the completion of the swing. I call the completion of these movements the "Kodak Moment."

On Preferences

Physically and mentally, everybody is different. That's why I say how you swing the golf club will always be unique. Your preferences are virtually unlimited. Just look at the Tour players. Some of the greatest champions brake almost every rule in the training manual. Yet they still succeeded and went on to become stars. How?

They "preferred" to create a movement for themselves that, even though it required much *compensation*, they could repeat the movement and regularly return the club to the ball in the desired, identical position. They developed a consistent shot pattern.

Notwithstanding these little idiosyncrasies, however, there were certain absolutes and essentials (you've head them called "fundamentals") that had to be followed. In fact, every golf legend incorporated "The Universals," "The Absolutes" and "The Five Essentials" I explain below.

The Universals

Every sport has its "Universals." To make a turn, a snow skier must transfer his or her weight to the right ski or the left. If a pitcher wants to throw a strike in baseball, he or she must manipulate the ball to somehow enter the strike zone.

The following are what I consider the "Universals" for the game of golf. I won't go into detail here, but you'll see them resurface again and again

The golf swing will not be the same for any two people, although there are certain principles, rules and prerequisites that will always remain constant, regardless of who's holding the club. I call these universal principles "The Universals"; I call the absolute rules governing those principles, "The Absolutes"; and the essential prerequisites of those rules, "The Essentials."

... Stay In The Mind

throughout the book. Many may seem obvious, but the human mind is tricky. What looks logical on paper often takes on a whole new meaning when you get to the first tee.

Universal #1: The ball is struck by a player using hand-eye coordination and motor skills.

Hand-eye coordination is a key component to striking the ball well.

No matter what kind of club or ball you use, no matter what you paid for your golf bag, no matter how much the green fee . . . you, and you alone, are what will make the ball soar. And as difficult as it may seem, hitting a golf ball correctly is actually much less complicated than driving a car and takes about as much physical and mental talent as riding a bike. Ever done either one of those?

I can't help you with hand-eye coordination — your "motor skills," as the medical people call them. You've already developed these. Some of us obviously have better ones than others. However, by learning proper body and club positions and movements, your motor skills will be strengthened as you learn to swing the club in a more efficient manner.

Universal #2: Ball-flight patterns and their causes must be understood.

This takes a little experience in hitting golf balls. Let's get back to the car. If you suddenly hear a pop, see rubber flying in your rearview mirror, and the car starts veering to the left, you can be pretty sure you've blown your left front tire.

The path your ball will take when struck will be the direct result of one or more of these factors. ☞

The same is true in golf. Illustrated below are the nine horizontal ball-flight patterns you'll see. These patterns are the direct result of conditions created during Impact by:

◆ Club path direction
◆ Clubface position in relation to the club path
◆ Angle of approach
◆ Impact location of ball on the clubface
◆ Clubhead speed upon Impact

I know this sounds like a great deal to consider and understand, but we'll be returning to these characteristics throughout the book. We might as well take fifteen minutes to learn them now.

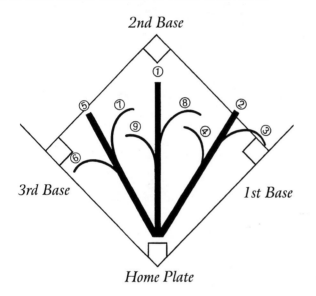

2nd Base

3rd Base

1st Base

Home Plate

HORIZONTAL BALL FLIGHT PATTERNS

1. Straight —The ball starts straight on the target line and does not curve as the ball travels forward.
2. Push —The ball starts to the right of the target line and remains in a straight direction.
3. Push Fade — The ball starts to the right of the target line, then continues to curve to the right of the target line.
4. Draw — The ball starts to the right of the target line, then curves gently back toward the target line but does not cross it.

Like most vocabulary terms, those used to denote ball flight patterns provide you with at least two very important things: (1) a quick, useful word to describe a complex relationship of causes and effects; and (2) the power, through your ability to readily identify that relationship, to do something about it — in this case, to improve your ball's flight pattern in accordance with the principles we'll be discussing throughout this book.

... Stay In The Mind

5. Pull — The ball starts to the left of the target line and continues in a straight direction.

6. Pull Hook — The ball starts to the left of the target line and curves abruptly further left, away from the target line.

7. Slice — The ball starts to the left of the target line, then curves abruptly toward the right and crosses the target line.

8. Tail-Away Slice — The ball starts on the target line then, after regaining roundness, curves right.

9. Tail-Away Hook — The ball starts on the target line, then, after regaining roundness, curves left.

Universal #3: A good golf swing is any movement you can repeat, has rhythm, balance and produces the desired shot ... with minimum compensation.

There exists no one "correct" way to swing a golf club. In striving to create our own "perfect" swing, we all must compensate to a greater or lesser degree. Just remember: The less compensation, the better.

That last part is critical. We all compensate. Some folks say Napoleon tried to conquer the world to compensate for the fact he was short. (My personal opinion is that he should have spent more time on the golf course. Ever notice how many of the best Tour players, with some notable exceptions, aren't very tall?)

If you jam your toe on a chair while going for that first cup of coffee in a dark kitchen, you favor the foot with the jammed toe as you make your way — more carefully — to the coffee pot. You compensate.

Maybe your wrists aren't quite as flexible as they used to be. You have to make some sort of compensation in your golf swing. You can't perform the perfect golf swing (this is true of Tour players as well as weekend golfers) so you learn to adjust. We must compensate for our uniqueness; we simply want to keep the compensation to a minimum.

Lessons That Rhyme ...

Universal #4: Hands determine the clubface position.

That's simple enough. If some people tried to hold a glass of iced tea the way they try to hold a golf club, they'd spill tea all over themselves every time they tried to take a drink. The position of your hands determines whether or not you'll get the tea out of the glass and into your mouth. Think about it.

Universal #5: Shoulder alignment upon Impact (and the use of hands and body parts to get there) influence forward club-path direction.

Take baseball again. You're a righthander and want to hit it to right field. You align your shoulders in that direction. Simple?

Universal #6: The golf ball only responds to the club during Impact.

You can do the Carolina "shag" before you hit the ball and pray to your Creator in the Backswing all you want. The ball will simply sit there, awaiting instructions from your clubface. Which leads me to:

Universal #7: IMPACT is the most important part of the golf swing. See chapter 9.

Universal #8: Your swing motion will be unique.

Look at Arnold Palmer. Chi Chi Rodriguez. Look at Greg Norman. Look at yourself. Your body, your ability, your experience are different than everyone else's. We are individuals. How we get there is where the fun begins.

Universal #9: The ball does not know who you are.

The golf ball may be the most democratic, politically correct item on the face of the earth. It doesn't care if you are male or female. It does not care about your religion, race, color, sex or creed. It doesn't care what you do for a living. It doesn't know which tee you're hitting from. *Attention ladies!* The golf ball

The position and use of the hands and movement of the shoulders will have a direct impact upon how well you strike the ball.

As we'll discuss in greater detail in chapter 10, "Impact" is comprised of three phases — contact, compression, and separation. In five ten-thousandths of a second (the time your ball and the clubface will spend together on any one swing), the fate of your shot will be decided.

... Stay In The Mind

See Appendix A at the back of this book for a "tear away" copy of the universals. ☞

will afford you the same courtesy (or disdain) it affords your husband, son, brother or significant other. The golf ball is equality in its purest form.

These are the "Universals." Put a copy in your office, kitchen or garage. I'd tell you to put it in your car, but I don't want to be responsible for accidents. I know golfers.

The Absolutes

During Impact, there are certain governing forces that will never change. Understanding what these forces are and how they can affect your ball's trajectory is an important first step in both evaluating and improving the success of your swing movement.

There is one area of the golf swing that, no matter who you are or how you swing, remains absolute: *Impact,* where the clubhead and ball collide. I don't care if you're John Daly, Jack Nicklaus, Nancy Lopez or Joe (Joanne) Smith, the following five "Absolutes" are etched in stone by the laws of physics. There are no secrets here.

1. ABSOLUTE: Clubface position aligned with the forward club-path direction.

RESULT: Ball flight is straight (without side spin) or curved (with side spin).

TRANSLATION: If the clubface meets the ball and is aligned perpendicularly at the proper time to the direction the clubhead is moving, the ball will travel straight.

However, if the clubface is not aligned perpendicularly at the proper time during Impact, and in the direction the clubhead is traveling, the result will be side spin . . . and the ball will curve. This is based on the laws of force and motion.

2. ABSOLUTE: The spot on the clubface where the ball should be struck.

RESULT: Maximum energy transfer (struck on the "sweet spot").

TRANSLATION: I know there's been a great deal of talk about the "sweet spot" being lower, higher or bigger due to clubhead design. Let's simplify. Think of it as the middle of the clubface. (Again, for the technology buffs, the "sweet spot" is the center of the mass on the clubface.)

Now think of a baseball pitcher. He (or she) tries to transfer all the energy of the windup into the hand that's throwing the ball. You're doing the same thing, only you've got a club between you and the ball.

3. ABSOLUTE: Importance of forward direction of the club path.

RESULT: Influences ball's starting direction (if the clubface alignment permits).

TRANSLATION: Think of a fisherman (woman) casting. When you cast, the tip of the pole should be traveling in the direction of where you want your line to start its journey. In golf, you move the clubhead toward the direction you want to ball to start. (Ever wonder why so many Tour players like to fish?)

4. ABSOLUTE: Importance of clubhead's angle of approach in relation to the ball.

RESULT: Height of the ball is created by the rate of backspin.

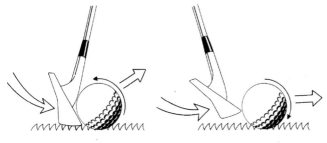

The angle at which the clubface strikes the ball will determine the ball's flight altitude. If it is struck below its equator with a downward motion, "backspin" will occur, allowing the ball's dimpled surface to increase its "lift" and "carry." If struck above its equator and/or with an upward motion, the ball will not become airborne.

TRANSLATION: This is where those grooves on your clubhead and the dimples on the ball come into play. If your clubface contacts the ball below its equator (think of the golf ball as the earth) while it's on its way down, this causes the ball to spin backwards (referred to as "backspin"). The combination of backspin (most important) and dimples (somewhat important) gets the ball airborne.

... Stay In The Mind

If your angle of approach isn't coming down steep enough to strike the ball with the clubface below the equator of the ball, there will be no backspin. The result is a "topped shot" (over-spin or top-spin), commonly referred to as a "worm burner."

5. ABSOLUTE: Importance of clubhead velocity.

RESULT: Distance. If the four Absolutes above are executed correctly, the velocity of your clubhead will determine the distance your ball will travel.

TRANSLATION: Think of the baseball pitcher and the fisherman (woman) again. The more velocity that pitcher can summon in his or her arm, the more "whip" that fisherperson can give the rod, the faster the pitch, and the further the bait will be thrown. Clubhead speed equals distance.

The Essentials

In addition to the "Universal" principles of the golf swing and the "Absolute" rules governing their application, the "Essentials" must be well understood if you are to put into practice what we'll be learning in theory.

I can hear it now. I remember one of my students (a golfer for forty-odd years) tell me, "I don't need any fundamentals. I need a good golf swing." I asked him what he was shooting. He told me 125 per eighteen holes. "Well, we don't want fundamentals to get in the way of that kind of score," I replied. After a moment's hesitation he relented: "Ok, I'll listen to a couple fundamentals — but no more!"

He listened to a couple and a couple more. Now he's enjoying his game — and his 9 handicap.

I listened too. The word "fundamentals" didn't say it all for me. I wanted something stronger, more all-encompassing. So in my teaching I've elevated "fundamentals" to something more dramatic, more important. I call them "Essentials." You need a good understanding of the *essential* parts of the golf swing and a certain comfort level with each one before you can attack your handicap.

I'm going to give you a brief synopsis of these five essentials to get you started. Then we'll look at

Lessons That Rhyme ...

some common problem areas golfers experience and apply the essentials to them. You've had enough of those "fundamentals?" Well, I treat them slightly differently, so you might want to take a look.

1. *Grip* . . . holding the handle. The golf club has four important parts: handle or grip, shaft, clubhead and clubface. Our hands are our link to the golf ball via the club. Hands hold, sense, feel and communicate. Hands determine the clubface position.

2. *Stance, alignment* . . . the position of your feet, knees, hips and shoulders in relation to the target line. Your stance influences club-path direction. *The shoulders are the most important body part to align parallel to the target line!*

3. *Posture* . . . arrangement of body parts. Sometimes I think golf instructors sound like biology teacher with all these "parts." All good ball-strikers have seven common traits when it comes to their posture when addressing the ball. That doesn't mean they all look the same — remember: Personal preferences are unlimited.

♦ Long neck or "chin up"
♦ Tilt forward from hips
♦ Weight evenly distributed on inside balls
    and heels of both feet
♦ Arms hang
♦ Elbows parallel to the target line
♦ Big chest
♦ Non-vertical (inclined) spine

4. *Club positions, especially during Impact.* Knowing the position of your club shaft, clubhead and clubface should be during the golf swing is important. Knowing where the club must be during Impact to produce the desired shot is paramount.

5. *Body and club relationships during the swing.* Finally, you must know the relationships that occur during the swing motion between your body and

Knowing your body's position before and during the swing motion is every bit as important as knowing your clubface's position. The swing must be repeatable, and the body is the key to achieving that repetition.

... Stay In The Mind

club, realizing that they won't be the same as everyone else's. Emphasis is placed on balance, rhythm and natural movements. We'll combine these with learned positions to produce your best swing with a minimum of compensation.

Now That We're Speakin' the Same Language . . .

We've discussed a lot of terms and concepts in this section. Don't worry if they seem a little unclear to you. In the following pages, we'll be putting them to work!

The next several chapters are all about the golf swing. As we have said, the swing motion has four components, or parts — the "Backswing," the "Downswing," the "Forwardswing" and the "Up-and-Around-Swing." The Backswing must be learned; the Downswing understood; the Forwardswing is natural; and the Up-and-Around-Swing is the result of everything that preceded it.

Many of my new students at Golf Meadows come to me after they've tried to emulate various theories and have become totally lost in technical details. That won't happen here; I've already gotten as technical as I'm going to get. It's all downhill from here.

Golf is a game. It should be fun. To my way of thinking, even learning it should be fun. The technical details should be left to gatherings of teaching professionals as we discuss various swing planes, shaft stiffness and other ways to make the game enjoyable.

That being said, I've got to say this: If you read nothing else in *Lessons That Rhyme*, read the next chapter. I really think it can change your entire game — permanently — for the better.

"Center of Balance," the topic of chapter 1, has not been given the high priority I believe it deserves among golf professionals. I put it here — at the "real" beginning of the book — because every other Essential in subsequent chapters depends upon this one movement.

Lessons That Rhyme ...

Chapter 1: COB

How To Throw Your Weight Around

Beware the Three-Legged Elephant

"Charlie, I feel like a three-legged elephant out there," Dr. D told me when he arrived for his first lesson. He'd called me as a last resort. "I've got all the books and videos. I watch the pros on television. But nothing seems to work," he said. After eight years of playing, he admitted he'd broken a few clubs over his knee but had never broken one hundred on his score card.

I had him hit a few balls and saw with his first swing why nothing was working. Like the majority of golfers out there who can't get below the century mark, Dr. D fell back on his right foot when he hit the ball and looked like he was about to stumble backward. *This may be the greatest fault of all high-scoring golfers.*

Predictably, he hit a worm burner, topping the ball with all his might. On the course, the ball wouldn't have made it passed the forward tees.

His description of a three-legged elephant wasn't far off. Any golfer who does not know where his or her Center of Balance (COB) is, and what it does, will never properly transfer his or her weight in the correct direction during the golf swing. The golfer is doomed to errant shots. Here's your first rhyme to remember:

Improper transfer of the "Center of Balance" (COB) may be the single greatest fault of all high-scoring golfers. Conversely, its proper management will be your single greatest asset on the course.

... Stay In The Mind

THE PLAYER WHO SWINGS AND FALLS BACK . . .
WILL NEVER GET THE BALL ON TRACK!

From the Address position through the completion of the entire swing motion, a sense of balance of all body parts is critical to the success of your ability to develop a repeatable swing movement. Although everyone's swing movement will be different, balance is one of the commonalities that all good players possess. Whether you're on the tee, on the green or somewhere in between, COB always comes into play. This is how weight is transferred toward the target leg and foot. Of course, if you don't know your COB . . . beware of the three-legged elephant.

For Dr. D, and for you, too, I'd like to repeat what I mentioned in the Introduction: *"A good golf swing is any movement that you can repeat, has rhythm, balance and produces the desire shot . . . with minimum compensation."*

Every athlete requires balance — tennis players, quarterbacks and, of course, golfers.

Fortunately, a sense of balance isn't something you actually need to worry about. We're all born with it. There's a fancy medical term for our body's sensory mechanism that automatically works to ensure our balance if it is threatened. If you want to impress your friends, when they ask what you're working on as you are practicing on the practice tee, just tell them you are working on your *"pro-pri-o-septives."* I can assure you they'll leave you alone.

Just think for a moment: We started learning about balance when we first pulled ourselves up in the crib. When we first learned to walk we were learning where our COB was. We had the muscles.

We are all born with a sense of balance. Learning how to capitalize on it while on the course means learning how and when — during your own unique swing movement — to transfer your weight properly toward the target and your left foot.

We were just figuring out which way was up. If we didn't have this innate sense of balance, we would all go around falling flat on our faces.

Our COB is responsible for all weight transfer of the lower body in the golf swing. Why is weight transfer so important? Because it is responsible, in whole or in part, for consistency, distance and direction. Yes, it is *that* important.

Our COB can move all over the place if we let it. We can make it go backward, forward, in (toward the ball), out (away from the ball), up, down and around. But the only COB movement we want to see in the golf swing is a movement lateral and parallel toward the target.

Your ability to properly manage your COB will be a measure of your ability, in part, to repeat your individual swing movement and to establish swing consistency in your game.

Lateral? Sorry. Football fans, think of a lateral pass — a straight line. Our COB should never move back or down. It should never move toward or away from the ball. It should only move laterally and parallel to the target line. Won't that make life simple? We'll go into more detail about COB as it relates to specific parts of the swing a little later. Right now, let's take a look at the illustration on pages 4-5.

Your body's COB is located about four inches below your belly button, right in the middle of your hips. Now that you know where it is, let's see what we're supposed to do with it. I've given you eight check points for your COB on the next two pages (ignore the beams; we'll get to them on page 7).

1. *At Address:* Weight is evenly distributed on the inside balls and heels of both feet.

2. *Swing-A-Way:* As you swing the club away from the ball to begin your Backswing movement, your COB does not move!

3. *Completed Backswing:* The COB has not moved, although the hips have rotated slightly. They have been restricted, as the shoulders wind up

... Stay In The Mind

Phases of the COB: Where your Center of Balance Moves during the Full Swing

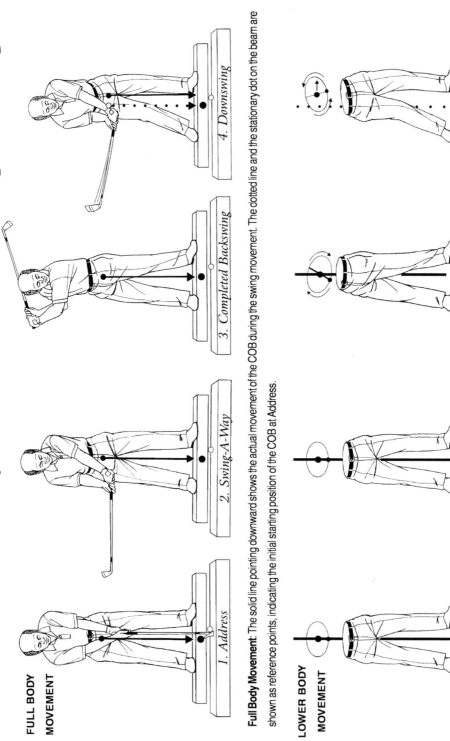

FULL BODY MOVEMENT

1. Address

2. Swing-A-Way

3. Completed Backswing

4. Downswing

Full Body Movement: The solid line pointing downward shows the actual movement of the COB during the swing movement. The dotted line and the stationary dot on the beam are shown as reference points, indicating the initial starting position of the COB at Address.

LOWER BODY MOVEMENT

1. Address

2. Swing-A-Way

3. Completed Backswing

4. Downswing

Lessons That Rhyme ...

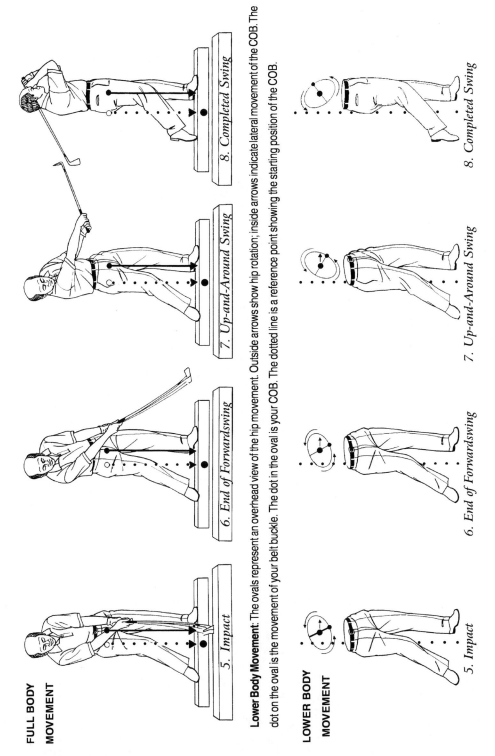

FULL BODY MOVEMENT

5. Impact   *6. End of Forwardswing*   *7. Up-and-Around Swing*   *8. Completed Swing*

Lower Body Movement: The ovals represent an overhead view of the hip movement. Outside arrows show hip rotation; inside arrows indicate lateral movement of the COB. The dot on the oval is the movement of your belt buckle. The dot in the oval is your COB. The dotted line is a reference point showing the starting position of the COB.

LOWER BODY MOVEMENT

5. Impact   *6. End of Forwardswing*   *7. Up-and-Around Swing*   *8. Completed Swing*

... Stay In The Mind

against a braced right leg due to the right knee's location.

4. *Downswing:* The Downswing is begun by the COB moving laterally as the hips begin to rotate, transferring the weight toward the left (or target) foot and moving the lower body in a direction parallel toward the target. This COB movement, along with proper hip rotation, is what starts the Downswing. *The lower body moves first.* The lateral movement of the COB begins toward the target as your hips begin to rotate. The lateral movement of the COB and the beginning rotation of the hips feel as though they move at the same time. Then your shoulders begin to unwind, following the lead of the hip rotation.

This is the most misunderstood movement in the entire golf swing. While you may not have been on a train in a while, either, think of that big old engine starting to move forward. It moves first — it has to — before the cars can. Then the chain reaction of the engine's movement starts everything else rolling. Your lower body is the engine.

5. *Impact:* The COB continues its lateral movement, parallel to the target line, toward the target as your weight continues to transfer onto your left (target) foot. You continue to rotate your hips while your shoulders follow that hip movement. Your lower body is leading the way and your upper body is responding, creating a powerful, balanced, graceful motion. (Notice I didn't say anything about the ball? We'll address this point in detail in chapter 4.)

6. *End of Forwardswing:* Hips and shoulders continue to unwind. COB continues its lateral, parallel movement toward the target.

7. *Up-and-Around Swing:* Your COB continues to move in a lateral, parallel direction toward the target. Your hips and shoulders continue their

The Downswing is another widely misunderstood facet of the golf swing. It begins with the lateral movement of the COB as the hip rotation and unwinding of the shoulders follow.

rotation and unwinding in a *circular direction* as the clubhead continues to travel in a more *upward direction.*

8. *Completed Swing:* This, my dear friends, is the "Kodak Moment." If your COB has moved laterally and parallel to the target line, and proper hip rotation has occurred, a "picture perfect" swing will result.

What's so great about this movement? You can *repeat it over and over again.* We're just having fun!

WHEN YOU'RE BALANCED THROUGHOUT THE SWING . . .
A REPEATABLE MOTION IS A SURE THING!

The Balance Beams

Some of us — maybe most of us — have a difficult time developing our sense of balance (our sense of COB) in our golf swing. Part of the problem is our natural tendency to "sway back" in the Backswing. We've also been told to "shift our weight from back to front" in the swing. I think that idea of "shifting" just adds to the swaying problem. I use the word "transfer" rather than "shift."

If balance is one of my student's problems, I put him or her on my "balance beams." Olympic gymnasts inspired me here. My "balance beams" are a pair of three 2" x 6" boards, four feet long, nailed together, about the size of railroad ties. The student stands on one beam and we place the other beam where the ball would be, forming the target line (refer to pages 4 and 5 for illustrations).

Then I have them start practice swinging. Yes, at first, you'll fee like Dr. D's three-legged elephant. You'll lose balance and come off the beam. (By the way, in losing your balance and coming off the

The Balance Beam exercise is Center of Balance management in its purest form: If you fail to move your COB in the proper direction, you will find yourself no longer standing on the beam.

. . . Stay In The Mind

beam, you're demonstrating that same innate ability to keep in balance that we talked about earlier!) But soon you'll be doing the full swing on the beam and staying there. You'll start hitting balls off the other beam. It always surprises me how quickly students get a sense of proper movement of their COB on the beams. (It's also a great way to check your posture; more on this in chapter 5.)

Now here's a little ditty to help remedy that tendency to "sway back." It's something of a band-aid, but it will help you keep your COB in the proper place *in the Backswing:*

**IF YOU DON'T WANT THE COB TO MOVE AT ALL …
POINT YOUR RIGHT FOOT AT OR AHEAD OF THE BALL!**

By pointing your right foot at or ahead of the ball, you guard against the spurious "sway back."

At Address, aim the toes on your right (i.e., back) foot at or ahead of the ball. Try it. You may feel

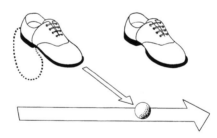

a little strange at first. But turning that foot will restrict your COB from moving back.

Just a friendly reminder: Proper weight transfer is responsible, in whole or in part, for consistency, distance and direction. The movement of your COB has everything to do with weight transfer. Get to know it. Get to understand it. Your COB will be the best friend you'll have in the golf swing. It allows gravity to work for you.

Chapter 2: Get A Grip

Good Golf Begins With a Good Grip

While most golf instruction books start off with the grip, I've never felt that it fully receives the amount of attention it deserves. If the hands are improperly placed in a manner not compatible with our unique swing motion, it's impossible for our swing motion to be completely successful. Our hands *hold, sense, feel* and *communicate*. They tell our mind where the club is and what the club is doing. Since our hands determine the clubface position throughout the swing, a good grip is critical to success.

There are three types of basic grips: overlapping, interlocking and ten-finger. I don't care which one you use, and everybody's grip is going to be a little different. Trevino's grip is not Nicklaus' grip is not Azinger's grip is not Palmer's grip. It has to do with strength, hand size, preference and flexibility. But every consistent ball-striker's grip has three commonalities:

1. The handle lays in the fingers more than in the palm. On the lesson tee at Golf Meadows I use a golf glove, like the one seen here, to demonstrate this principle. If you can see the dot in your reflection in the mirror, the handle is in the fingers. If the dot is covered, it's in the palm. The handle in the fingers allows the club to rotate naturally during the swing. Here's a rhyme to help you:

Basic Grips:

Overlapping Grips: The little finger of the right hand is placed over the space between the index and third finger of the left hand.

Interlocking Grip: The little finger on the right hand and index finger of the left hand entwine, locking the hands together. These fingers do not touch the handle.

Ten Finger Grip: All ten fingers touch the handle when holding the club.

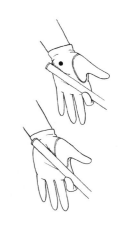

... Stay In The Mind

SEE THE DOT . . . AND IMPROVE YOUR SHOT!

2. The second way to check yourself is what I call "The Split." Good ball-strikers have a split between the index and middle finger of the right hand when holding the handle. When there's a split, the handle is in the fingers; no split and it's in the palm. It doesn't matter what kind of grip you have, the split must be there.

IF YOU DON'T SEE THAT SPLIT . . .
THE RIGHT HAND DOESN'T FIT!

3. Finally, all consistent ball-strikers simply hold the handle as they swing and let gravity work its magic. Because of supple wrists (more on this later), natural rotation of the forearms will occur. Gravity makes this happen. Inconsistent players must use their hands to hit the ball because their body, club, or some combination of the two is out of position. It starts with an improper grip. Here are two reminders:

HIT THE BALL WITH YOUR HANDS . . .
AND YOU'LL NEVER KNOW WHERE IT LANDS!

HOLD THE HANDLE AS YOU SWING . . .
LET GRAVITY DO EVERYTHING!

If the position of the clubface is in the correct alignment at the beginning of the swing, it's going to return and be correct during Impact — if you allow gravity to do its job. More about gravity later.

Remember, good players don't hit with their hands. They just hold on to the handle as they swing.

Lessons That Rhyme ...

Chapter 3: Hang Loose

Wrists Hinge, Arms Swing

Wrists

A first-time student of mine and I were getting along just fine. Her hands were placed on the handle as though she were a par shooter. She was an excellent tennis player but had decided to add golf to her repertoire following her husband's retirement. "If I want to see more of him, it will have to be on the golf course," she told me one fine morning.

"Well, that's really nice," I said. A Carolina wren was singing sweetly.

"I don't want to be nice. I want to beat him," she replied. "Now, where do I cock my wrists? My husband's always talking about cocking his wrists."

There's been a great deal written and said about the "wrist cock" or "setting the wrists." Well, the truth is, the left wrist does cock and the right wrist hinges. To be honest, I don't even like to use the word "cocking"; I prefer hinge and unhinge. Cocking sounds too rigid and static, and there's nothing rigid or static

Your wrists provide a natural hinge between your club and arms. Everything your body does in preparing to strike the ball will be both communicated and magnified by this hinging motion.

... Stay In The Mind

Gravity is the most constant force on earth. What better force to rely upon when trying to develop a repeatable swing motion? Remember, all you do is hold the club. Gravity does the rest.

about the golf swing. It also complicates matters. Let me give you a mental picture of what the wrists do as the arms swing.

Wrists provide a natural hinge between your hands and arms. When you're swinging a golf club, they create a two-lever mechanism as the arms are swung. This hinging and unhinging multiplies clubhead speed. We must allow our friend gravity — and not us — to make the lever action work.

I call gravity "our friend" because it is the most consistent force on earth. It never changes. Rather than setting or cocking the wrists, we must let gravity determine the consistency of the lever action that will return the club to the ball the same way every time.

Speaking of repeating, I can't say it often enough: *A good golf swing is any movement you can repeat, has rhythm, balance and produces the desire shot . . . with a minimum of compensation.*

Of course, we can treat our friend gravity unkindly by moving our hands and arms all over the place. We can also keep our wrists from doing their thing by locking (or "cocking" or "setting") them in place, either hinged, unhinged or somewhere in between. But the best way to keep wrist movement natural and flowing is to make sure the wrists remain supple and limber.

Look at Tom Watson's wrists. He just lets it happen. All good ball-strikers allow gravity and the weight of the club to make their wrists hinge and unhinge. These two rhymes ought to help you out:

WRISTS THAT ARE TIGHT . . . DESTROY BALL FLIGHT!

WRISTS THAT ARE LIMBER . . .
KEEP YOU OUT OF THE TIMBER!

Arms

My tennis-playing student picked up on this right away. (She also now posts, on a regular basis, lower golf scores than her husband.)

Arms swing; they are not pulled through, pulled down or guided along. They simply swing. They either respond to the movement of the body, or the body responds to the movement of the arms. Most players should simply swing their arms and allow the body to respond to the movement the arms create.

Get yourself in front of a mirror. Tilt your spine slightly forward by bending from the hips, keeping your spine somewhat straight. Let your arms hang down, limp. Now swing them back and forth together. Stay loose. Stay flexible. That's the feeling I want you to have when you swing the club. Stay "soft."

Without a club, put your hands together, palm to palm. Allow the right palm to face the target. Now, take several practice swings, moving through all four areas of the swing. Recall the Backswing, Downswing, Forwardswing, and the Up-and-Around Swing.

What do your forearms do while your arms are swinging during the Forwardswing and into the Up-and-Around Swing? The forearms cross, don't they?

While moving through the Forwardswing and into the Up-and-Around Swing, notice that the right forearm crosses over the left.

... Stay In The Mind

Wrists are not "stiff" at any time during the golf swing. Stiffness causes tension; it complicates our ability to reproduce a consistent swing motion, and it slows down our clubhead speed, taking distance off our shot.

Let them.

Now place the handle of the club properly in your hands (see chapter 2) and swing. This could be your "magic move to success." Don't try to guide the club. The right forearm crossing over the left makes the hands rotate (which means the clubface will correct during Impact). Let them. Don't try to direct the ball. Just let the miracle happen!

One of the biggest problems golfers have is allowing the wrists and arms to become stiff. This stiffness causes tension throughout our body. I suspect it all started when you were told to keep that left arm "stiff" in the Backswing. Sure, it's got to be extended. It looks straight — but it's not stiff. Stiff arms slow down our swing, and that takes distance off the ball. The medical profession tells us you can move up to 30% faster with relaxed muscles. You can swing faster with soft arms — and that adds distance! All good ball-strikers have soft arms.

Remember, hands are made to hold, arms are made to swing, wrists are made to hinge. *Gravity* makes the club come down. Let's look at a few rhymes to help you "hang loose."

THE SOFTER YOUR ARMS AND SHOULDERS CAN BE ...
THE GREATER YOUR CLUBHEAD'S VELOCITY!

LET THE FOREARMS CROSS ...
SHOW THE BALL WHO'S BOSS!

Chapter 4: Custom Placement

The "Fitting" Formula for Ball Location

What's that they say in the real estate business? You just need to know three words: "location, location, location." Well, finding the right ball location for your swing is just as critical in the golf business. I realize that virtually all the books and videos out there have told you about a specific spot to place the ball. That would be just fine . . . if everyone had the perfect swing and we were all built the same. But we know that's just not the case.

No two golfers' swing moments will be the same, nor will their golf balls' location at Address. In determining where to place your

If everyone's swing is going to be different, ball position has to be different, too. Every good ball-striker has his or her favorite spot. You'll have to experiment to find out just where yours is — but you don't have to experiment without a clue. The ball's location will always be somewhere between the middle of your feet to slightly inside your left heel.

There are two primary factors that influence the ball location for your personal swing: hand position on the handle, and the speed of your COB movement.

ball, let's consider hand position and the speed of your COB movement.

Hand Position

Let's go back to our mirror. With your club, face the mirror and assume the

... Stay In The Mind

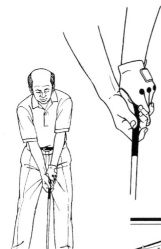

Address position. Your first check is the number of knuckles you see on your left hand. Now, lift the club so the shaft is horizontal to the ground. Look in the mirror. Count the knuckles. The more knuckles you can see, the further back your ball location should be. The opposite is true, too. The less knuckles, the further forward your ball location should be. That's step number one. Here's a rhyme that will help:

THE MORE KNUCKLES YOU SEE . . .
THE FURTHER BACK THE BALL MUST BE!

👆 *The more knuckles you can see in the mirror as you hold the club, the further back your ball location should be at Address. The less knuckles, the further forward.*

The quicker your COB moves, transferring your weight toward the target (& left foot), the further forward the ball must be. ☞

COB Movement

We've talked at great length about weight transfer and COB, but at this point we need to talk about them just a little more. Think of the COB movement as the transferring of your weight *from* the location at the completed Backswing *toward* the front (target foot) as you perform the Downswing and

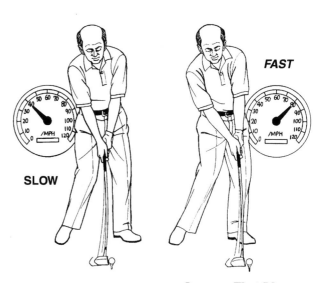

SLOW

FAST

Forwardswing. The faster the weight transfers toward your target foot, the more forward your ball location should be. Here's a rhyme:

THE QUICKER YOUR COB TRANSFER ON THE TEE ...
THE FURTHER FORWARD YOUR BALL MUST BE!

By the way, this is true anywhere a full swing is performed — not just on the tee.

Tee Height

Number of knuckles and speed of COB movement determine tee height. Again, this is a personal preference and depends on your individual swing. Some golfers like to tee it high. Others sink it to almost ground level. There is no wrong height for teeing up the ball, but there is a right one — the one that works with your swing. However, as I mentioned, the ball should be placed somewhere from the middle of your foot location to a point just inside your left heel.

Experiment with a few tee heights before settling on one. The number of knuckles you see, the speed of the COB, and the height of your tee will all determine where the ball should be.

THE HIGHER YOUR TEE ...
THE FURTHER FORWARD YOUR BALL MUST BE!

Chapter 5: Posture
You Should've Listened To Your Mother

Your posture will be different from everyone else's, but all good posture allows for a more rapid transfer of the COB and will help you maintain a consistent, flowing swing. Good posture guards against unnecessary injuries that could land you on your back in bed ... and away from the course.

Posture is simply the arrangement of our body parts at the Address position. (Sounds like we're back in Anatomy 101 again.) I think of all the times I've walked up and down the lesson tee and looked at the painful expressions of golfers as they address the ball. Some of them could put the circus contortionist to shame.

Posture may not sound too exciting (you just want to get out there and hit the ball!) but that's what good posture will allow you to do. It facilitates a more rapid transfer of the COB and will help you maintain a consistent, flowing swing. It will also keep you from hurting yourself.

I suspect that a great deal of these strange positions are due to all the "swing hints" you may have picked up over the years while standing over the ball — hints like, "Squat like your sitting on a bar stool," or "Level those shoulders."

It's time for the mirror again.

Let's go back to one of our Universal statements: your swing will be unique. If your swing is unique, your posture will also be unique, to a degree. Not everyone will look like Davis Love III or Annika Sorenstam. The only person you'll look like is you. Your body is different. Your arms may be shorter or longer. You may be more or less flexible. You may be as trim as a twelve-year-old, or it could be that the "middle-age spread" has, well, spread. That means we have to compensate for our individual bodies. But good posture allows you to swing the club with a minimum of compensation.

With that in mind, here are seven common universal traits for fostering good posture in your setup:

1. *Long Neck or "Chin Up."* You might have a neck like Audrey Hepburn or one like a lineman for the Green Bay Packers. It doesn't matter. I just want you to think "long neck." It will help you keep your chin up, creating clearance between chin and chest.

You can also think of that of that nice English phrase, "chin up." If you keep your chin up, you'll create that "long neck." Remembering this phrase when you're down two at your company's annual golf tournament with only three holes left might help you in a number of ways.

2. *Tilt forward from your hips.* Too many golfers bend from the waist. If you do this, your back will appear curved in the shoulder area. Look in your mirror. It's impossible to properly begin the Swing-A-Way motion from this position; the remaining movements and positions during the swing would contain more compensation than is necessary. So tilt forward from your hips, allowing your spine to create a somewhat straight line.

3. *Weight evenly distributed.* Make sure all your weight is equally distributed to the inside balls and heels of both feet. This is true for just about every sport I can think of. A boxer keeps his weight there to maintain balance and strength before he throws

Follow these seven "posture traits" to ensure a minimum amount of compensation in your swing. Remember, even the best swing — the longest drive, the most accurate chip shot — won't excuse inconsistency elsewhere on the course. Everyone gets lucky every now and then. You want repetition, not roulette.

... Stay In The Mind

Like many practice techniques discussed in this book, "practicing" good posture (both in front of the mirror and on the course) will not only lower your golf score, but will provide you with a better understanding of what is happening during your swing, empowering you to correct any problems, should one occur.

a punch. Watch a tennis player waiting to receive a serve.

If you live near the beach (or a sand bunker), try this: Stand barefoot in the sand in your Address position. Now back off and look to see the impression your feet made. Is the deepest impression in the area where the inside balls and heels of both feet were located? If not, try again until they are!

4. *Arms Hang.* We talked about this in chapter 3. Don't push your elbows into your side. Just let them hang loose alongside your chest.

5. *Elbows in line.* Both elbows should be parallel to the target line, or the intended line of flight.

6. *Big chest.* Remember the Tarzan movies with Johnnie Wisemiller beating his chest? Do it as a reminder! I don't care if you're shaped like Dolly Patton or Don Knox, golfers must think "big chest." Remember your mother telling you not to slouch your shoulders? She was right.

7. *Inclined spine.* When you hold a golf club, your right hand will be approximately six inches lower than your left. This is going to cause your right shoulder to become lower than your left, and your spine to incline toward the right. That's just natural. If you try to keep it vertical, you'll begin your swing with a "chicken wing" already in place — not a good start. Look in the mirror again and you'll see what I mean.

Keeping these seven steps in mind might sound a little complicated, but I guarantee that if you get in

Lessons That Rhyme ...

front of your mirror and practice the correct posture a few minutes each day, it will soon come as naturally to you as walking . . . or dancing (more on this in the next chapter).

Good posture tells you how far you stand away from the ball. It's about the same posture with every club, from the driver to the sand wedge, for the full swing. Most inconsistent players tend to reach, causing them to bend from the waist, not the hips. They can't keep their chin up or have a long neck or a big chest. When you're too far away, you start to rock and sway, and your swing falls apart.

Another way of looking at it: Good posture will dictate how near you should stand to the ball. As golfing great Gene Sarazen once said, "You can't stand too near the ball while hitting it."

Here are some rhymes to help your posture.

Your posture "informs" your swing by telling you how far away from the ball you should stand. Once developed, good posture won't change from shot to shot, regardless of the club used; it will remain — and will help your entire swing remain — consistent.

ALL GOOD PLAYERS, AT ADDRESS . . .
HANG THEIR ARMS BESIDE THEIR CHEST!

IF YOUR CAUGHT SQUATTIN' . . .
YOUR SHOT WILL BE ROTTEN!

... Stay In The Mind

Chapter 6: Sorrell Waltz
The "Perfect 10" Approach

Remembering the movements that conspire to create a successful swing is as simple as remembering nine words and one phrase.

It happens every day at the school. I have a beginner's clinic going. A dozen faces look expectantly up at me as I go through some foundation work about the Essentials. Then I pause (I like to think of it as a "dramatic pause") and say, "I would like to end your confusion and frustration. *The entire golf swing can be understood and performed when you know and can act on nine words and one phrase.* That's it! A perfect 10!

That's when I hear the chorus, "But Charlie!"

I promised you I would keep it simple. I think this is as simple as it gets: *99% of all golfers in this world can have a consistent, successful golf swing by remembering nine words plus one phrase.* We can talk all day and night about the different parts of the swing, but the entire swing movement boils down to something requiring a lot less effort to learn.

As you have already read (or will soon read) there are certain commonalities I stress about the swing and the Address position. They're worth repeating here:

♦ The Impact position and the Address position are not the same.

♦ All parts of the body must work in harmony and in balance.

♦ A good position at Address creates the conditions that allow swing movements that require the least amount of compensation. A good Address includes a good grip, good stance (alignment) and proper posture.

♦ The COB relates to lower-body movements. However, these movements also influence upper-body motion.

♦ Once the arms begin their gradual acceleration in the Downswing, this acceleration continues until the "Kodak Moment" is achieved. That is when the swing movement is complete.

♦ For the proper sequence of events to take place, remember: The COB doesn't move in the Backswing. Beginning with the Downswing, however, it does move laterally and parallel to the target line, toward the target until the swing movement is complete,

♦ For 99% of all golfers, the more tension-free your movement, the better your shot.

This is all fine and good . . . until you find yourself staring down a long par 5 fairway and everyone's waiting on you to swing. That's when you should take a deep breath, forget all the theory, and simply remember this:

☞ The "Perfect 10" — the simple solution to the golf swing in nine words and one phrase.

(1) **HANDS** . . . (2) **HOLD**
(3) **ARMS** . . . (4) **SWING**
(5) **WRISTS** . . . (6) **HINGE**
(7) **ELBOWS** . . . (8) **FOLD**, (9) **EXTEND**

And the phrase . . .

(10) **"THE BODY RESPONDS TO THE MOVEMENT OF THE ARMS" (99% OF GOLFERS), OR "THE BODY CREATES THE MOVEMENT OF THE ARMS" (1% OF GOLFERS).**

That's it?
That's it. Here's how it works.

... Stay In The Mind

Maintain your balance in the backswing and create a kind of "1-2-3-1" waltz rhythm: Make the Backswing movement in the 1-2-3 and return the clubhead to the ball on "1." My practice preference is Strauss' "Blue Danube" in three-quarter time.

Simply swing your arms back, free of tension. Hold on to the handle with your hands and allow your wrists to hinge whenever it feels natural to you.

Continue to swing the arms back and upward, feeling your shoulders respond, until you are ready for the Downswing. Attempt to keep the COB as near as possible to the position it was at Address.

When you have reached the completed Backswing, all parts should begin moving together into the Downswing, somewhat toward the target. The arms are swinging and the other parts of your body are responding to the movement of the arms. *Maintain your balance and create a kind of waltz rhythm.* You know, "1-2-3-1." Make the Backswing movement in the 1-2-3 and return the clubhead to the ball on "1."

For you music lovers, my practice preference is Strauss' "Blue Danube." It provides a perfect 1-2-3-1 cadence in three-quarter time. (I have yet to discover the appropriate "heavy metal" practice music.)

Continue the same rhythm sequence for all your shots and be sure that, when you hit the ball, more weight is on your left (target) foot than your right.

Practice hitting shots from fifty yards around the green. Learn to create different types of shots. Use your putter off the green when practical. I often tell students to putt when they can (you don't have to be on the green), chip when they can't putt, and pitch only when they have to. It's the same 1-2-3-1 cadence with your putter, too. You can become an 85 (or much less) shooter quickly, easily and consistently. I guarantee it!

Lessons That Rhyme ...

MOVE ALL PARTS IN HARMONY . . .
AND THE CLOSER TO PAR YOU'LL BE!

HANDS HOLD—ARMS SWING—WRISTS HINGE—
ELBOWS FOLD & EXTEND . . .
NINE WORDS AND ONE PHRASE MAKE YOUR SWING
A "PERFECT 10!"

Note to scratch players: Oh, yes, I can hear you ask: "Charlie, what about that 1%?" Dear golfers, 1% of you shoot par or better on a regular basis. You have no handicap. You play and practice often. Your swing is different because the body moves the arms.

However, to avoid confusion, I've included only the swing method that will work for the greatest majority of golfers. If you would like "The Par Shooter's Perfect 10," you'll have to wait for the second edition.

Chapter 7: The 'Plane' Truth

The Only Swing Plane You'll Ever Need

We now know that everyone's swing is unique, and the same applies to so-called "swing planes." Nevertheless, as we have seen with other variable facets of the swing movement, there are a few general principles that hold true regardless of who's holding the club.

"Charlie, which swing plane are we going to work on today?" my student asks. I am sorely tempted to say, "The one to Tulsa!" But I bite my tongue.

The swing plane is another one of the most misunderstood parts of the golf swing. There are more opinions about it than there are 747s that fly into JFK International.

My students know I'm an easygoing sort of fellow and prefer a smile to a scowl when a golfer nails one impressively to the right and nearly takes out my video camera (and a few of my other students). But I believe I show the greatest self-control when a student asks which of the swing planes he or she should concentrate on. That's when I know the golfer has been reading too much.

If you took five of the most talented ladies and gentlemen on Tour and tried to map out their "swing planes" throughout their swing, you would end up with a cartoonist's version of a twirling majorette's baton. Recall the little whirl at the top that Chi Chi does — or John Daly when he practically drops the clubhead on the ground at the end of his Backswing.

All these "plane" variations, if you remember our Universals, come about because every swing is unique. All those great ball-strikers nevertheless do have one swing plane in common. But first let's

Lessons That Rhyme ...

discuss a few basics.

A plane is simply a flat surface. The glass in a store window is a vertical plane. The floor you are standing on looking through that vertical plane (most likely at a new set of clubs), is a horizontal plane. Those planes are easy enough to understand because you can see and touch them.

The plane, as related to the golf swing, is also easy to understand and identify — once you know what to look for. It is determined by the angle formed by the club shaft in relation to the target line at any point during the swing or at Address.

I promised I would keep this book simple. This chapter may be the best example of that promise. There is only one swing plane you must create during the swing. Here it is: When the Forwardswing begins, the club shaft should be angled to align the handle-end of the club shaft toward the target line. The other end will be aligned at or slightly below the right shoulder. The hands are located along this same angle and should be about hip level. The *leading edge* of the club should also be aligned toward the target line, but at a different angle

A plane contains at least three noncollinear points. (opps ... sorry!!!!). If your swing were filmed so that the motions of the club shaft were blurred to show the club's path through the air, you would be looking at your individual swing plane.

This is the only swing plane you'll ever need to become a good player. Remember: the more compensation required for repetition, the greater the risk of mistakes.

... Stay In The Mind

The "leading edge" of the club is the club's front edge, at the bottom of the clubface.

than the club shaft. (see Chapter 9)

That's it. One plane, from the beginning of the Forwardswing to a point during the Up-and-Around Swing where your hands reach a point about hip high. The club shaft and leading edge should both be aligned to the target line at these check points.

The illustration on page 27 will help you see it. So will a mirror. Just concentrate on getting on the plane in your Forwardswing as quickly as possible. The rest will take care of itself.

Here are a few rhymes to keep in mind:

THINK ONE PLANE . . .
AND THE GREEN'S YOUR DOMAIN!

IF YOU'RE NOT ON PLANE . . .
THEY'LL NEVER KNOW YOUR NAME!

Chapter 8: The Swing Foundation

What the Feet and Knees Do

The Feet

Consider the feet. We buy nice shoes for them. On the golf course, we want them dry. We want them to hold out for eighteen holes (or more). We stand on them while waiting for our order at the 19th hole. We soak them, usually after thirty-six holes in one day. But what do they have to do with the golf swing?

Everything.

"Did you see that awful swing, Charlie?" a frustrated student of mine asked during practice one day.

"I wasn't looking at your swing," I replied. "I was looking at your feet." And I was: *They* were the problem, not the swing.

Your feet are, quite literally, the foundation of your golf swing. If they are correctly spaced, properly aligned with the target line and are responsive to the swing movement, there's a very good chance you'll hit the ball well.

One general thought: Be light on your feet. Remember the wonderful Fred Astaire and Ginger Rogers movies? Remember how they seemed to be walking on air — even when they were standing still? That's how I would like you to feel: *light*.

Here's what the feet do, and what should happen to them, throughout the swing:

A good golf swing does not neglect its foundation, the feet. How they are spaced and aligned — and how well they respond to the swing movement — will affect your entire game.

... Stay In The Mind

Initial Placement

☞ *Proper width, weight distribution and alignment of the feet ensure the foundation of your swing is as sound and constant as possible.*

Width. When the feet are the proper distance apart, they stabilize the legs in the Backswing. This allows them to move correctly throughout the reminder of the swing, keeping us in balance. What is the right width? Take a yardstick and measure from the middle of one shoulder joint to the other. Got the number? Now, lay the yardstick on the ground and mark off the distance with two golf tees. Place the inside of your heels outside of, but touching, the tees. That's it!

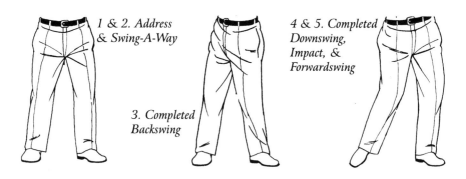

1 & 2. Address & Swing-A-Way

3. Completed Backswing

4 & 5. Completed Downswing, Impact, & Forwardswing

☝ *As we discussed in chapter 1, negotiating your COB is perhaps the most challenging facet of the golf swing. Here we more closely examine the role of the feet & knees in COB movement.*

Weight. At Address, distribute your weight evenly on the inside balls and heels of both feet. Remember chapter 5 (page 20) when you stood in the sand? Here it is again.

Alignment. Got your yard stick ready again?

1. Place it parallel to the target line, at approximately the distance you will be placing your feet in the Address position.

2. Place the toes of both shoes on the yardstick, with both feet aligned perpendicularly to the yardstick. (Because this exercise could be better depicted in the above illustrations *without* the yardstick, it was not included here.)

3. Keeping the left heel on the ground, lift your toe just enough to turn it out toward the target, about

four inches or 30 degrees. Why turn it? It has to do with weight transfer. (See below, "Swing Movement: COB Transfer").

4. Now your feet are aligned parallel to the target line, even though your left toe isn't on the line. Confusing? Yes, but true. You can only measure true alignment from the back of the heels, not the toes.

Swing Movement: COB Transfer

Right Foot. Keep the weight on the inside ball and heel (illustration phases 2 & 3). Don't move it, but keep it ready to respond to the swing motion. My

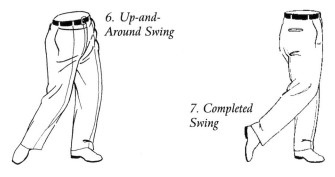

6. Up-and-Around Swing

7. Completed Swing

Notice the hip rotation and lateral (forward) movement of the COB during the Downswing (phase 4). In this forward movement, weight is transferred toward the left leg and foot.

frustrated student was allowing it roll to the outside, which moved back his COB! Ugly.

Left Foot. Your heel may come up slightly, and that's OK. Just make sure the COB doesn't move back!

When you begin to move your COB laterally (phases 4-7), you are transferring your weight toward your left leg and foot. Your right foot helps the transfer by pushing off, like a track runner on the blocks in the 100-meter dash. As your COB moves to the left, the left foot will begin to roll out on its left side (phases 4-6). This provides a balanced point to support the oncoming weight. That's why we turned the left foot outward (see "Alignment" on facing page).

... Stay In The Mind

The lateral movement of the COB culminates in the completed swing (phase 7), leaving your right foot on pointe and virtually "weightless."

Note: At the end of the swing (phase 7, page 31), the toe of your right foot should be barely touching the ground and almost all of your weight is on your left foot. The right toe of your shoe will be dragged forward from its original position in response to COB lateral movement. That's why Payne Stewart developed a line of metal-toed golf shoes — to protect his right toe as he dragged it across the turf!

You should feel no weight on the right foot when the swing movement is completed, only a sensation of balance. Try it.

Follow the illustrations on pages 30 and 31 until you get comfortable with it. That's what the feet do. Here are a couple rhymes to help:

BE LIGHT ON YOUR FEET . . .

AND YOUR SWING WILL REPEAT!

THE FLATTER THE FEET . . .

THE GREATER THE DEFEAT!

The Knees

My wife Joyce and I were sitting on the front porch of our house one summer evening looking out over beautiful Golf Meadows, sipping iced tea. It was dusk and I had just finished my last lesson for the day. Georgia crickets were beginning their nightly concert.

My bride said, "Charles, dear, there's something I'd like to ask."

"By all means," I replied, settling into the rhythm of the evening.

"Why do you have Post-It Notes on your knees?"

I looked down and, sure enough, two canary

yellow squares of sticky paper were stuck to my bare knees. Right in the center of each was a big black dot I had added for emphasis.

I will concoct just about any device, and tape, fold and mangle any part of my body to help a student become a better player. In my classroom, I have boxing gloves, baseball bats, an assortment of colored, felt-tipped markers that would be the envy of any kindergarten teacher, boxes of masking tape and more pads of those sticky little squares than one human being should be permitted to own. My wife was used to me coming home with various parts of my anatomy or clothing highlighted in some fashion, but the little squares with the black dots were new.

"That's so students can focus on my knees," I answered, pulling off the sticky pieces of paper.

"No offense, dear, but why would someone want to look at *your* knees?"

It was a good question (I ignored the sarcasm in her voice). Most golfers don't pay much attention to their knees unless they hurt or become absurdly out of place in the swing. But for our purposes, I would like to concentrate on the right knee. Remember the good posture we learned in chapter 5? Both knees are flexed at Address, like the short stop or tennis player.

What happens to the right knee in the Backswing?

Nothing. That's right, nothing. It should not move. However, it should remain flexed. By not moving, it keeps our COB from moving back. I like to think of it as a kind of governor for our Backswing. All good ball-strikers keep the right knee in approximately the same position as it was at Address. By not moving the right knee, it encourages us to swing

The right knee should not move during the Backswing. This prevents our COB from moving and acts as a "governor" to guide the path along which our arms and hands travel during the Backswing.

... Stay In The Mind

our arms and hands in the same direction, at the same speed, and to the same position until the completion of the Backswing.

If we straighten up the right knee, lock it, squat down or move it around in the Backswing, our club (and COB) can go anywhere! You'll never be able to make any two swings the same. Your shots will always be inconsistent.

Keeping the right knee in the same place also helps us develop hip resistance in the Backswing and, at the same time, readies us for the "push off" movement of the right foot and knee when we start to move our COB.

With the lateral movement of the COB, the right knee moves along and, at the Kodak Moment, will be pointing at or somewhat to the left of the target.

Keep the left knee flexed, at the ready position, and allow it to turn naturally in response to hip rotation as you complete the swing.

Now the left knee doesn't move much at all. Golfers have a problem with the left knee "kicking in" and away from the target. Rather than simply remaining flexed and ready to accept the transfer of weight when the COB moves, golfers sometimes allow the left knee to move too near the ball.

Proper knee position and movement will add a tremendous amount of consistency to your swing.

Here are two rhymes that sum it all up. Think of those little yellow pieces of paper:

IF YOUR RIGHT KNEE MOVES . . . YOU'RE SURE TO LOSE!

KEEP THE RIGHT KNEE ON THE SPOT . . .
IMPROVE YOUR SWING A LOT!

Chapter 9: Club Positions

"Check Points Charlie"

"What was that?" I asked my student. During a practice Backswing, he looked like he was trying to write a figure eight in the sky with his clubhead.

"That's a 'Figure Eight Move,'" he replied. "I watched this pro on TV and he nailed one with it." He stepped up to the ball. When he began his Downswing, the clubhead shot out, wobbled, made an erratic arc and crashed into the ball, which dribbled off the tee. My student looked up at me.

"Duck Hook Move," I replied.

If, in hopes of finding your "secret to success," you attempt to copy a pro on television who seems to have a "different" type of swing, I have just two words for you: Forget it! You will probably end up looking like a pretzel on the first tee. By the time you reach the second tee, it will take a considerable amount of effort on behalf of all the other players in your group to untangle you. You will succeed in executing every shot imaginable . . . except the one you want.

Yes, there are some amazingly different club and body positions that, in part, are effective for some Tour players. But we must always remember that these are some of the most talented, highly skilled professionals in the world. They are the

There are no quick-fix "secrets" to a successful golf swing — and we don't need any. Resist trying to "copy" someone else's swing movement. Try instead to keep your own compensations to a minimum. This chapter contains four "checkpoints" to help you.

... Stay In The Mind

exceptions that prove the rhyme. The ones who have developed those "amazingly different" golf swings nonetheless have spent countless hours reproducing the movement. It doesn't matter what compensations they need to make, or how complicated their movements, they are able to continually repeat their unique golf swing — under the pressure of tournament golf!

So let's put the pros aside for a moment. I promised to keep things simple. There are only four areas of the swing in which you should know the position of your club:

Here are the four "Check Points Charlie" — the four areas of the swing during which you should know the exact position of your club shaft and leading edge.

AREA 1. The completed Backswing.
AREA 2. Beginning for the Forwardswing.
AREA 3. When the hands are at hip level in the Up-and-Around Swing.
AREA 4. The Kodak Moment.

At these four positions, focus on just two parts of the golf club to keep compensations to a minimum: the club shaft and the leading edge.

At Golf Meadows, I try to define "leading edge" very clearly because it is of vital importance to club position. To this end, I've created a little training aid. You *can* (and I want you to) do this at home. It's like one of those projects you did in scouts or art class or shop. Supplies you'll need are:

Materials you'll need in the training aid. Chances are most of these are laying around the house.

♦ A 5/16" wooden dowel, three feet long.
♦ A roll of one-inch masking tape.
♦ An eight-foot piece of PVC pipe. (Note: You'll actually have to buy a ten-foot section, since they don't sell them eight feet long.)
♦ A two or three iron.
♦ Your mirror.
♦ A golf ball.

Lessons That Rhyme ...

Are you ready?

Position the dowel on the bottom of the club along the leading edge. With about one foot sticking out past the end nearest you as you hold the club at Address, and about two feet sticking out beyond the other end, attach the dowel to the clubhead by winding the tape around them three or four times. Make sure the dowel is perfectly aligned with the leading edge.

Regardless of the clubface position, you now have a very visual alignment-aid identifying the leading edge.

Now, lay the PVC pipe on the floor or ground to simulate the target line. We've mentioned earlier that everything in golf is based on the target line. Well, listen up — here we go!

Position yourself so your reflection in the mirror will show your right side, as though it were a person looking down your target line.

Check the position of the target line. Assume your Address position, with the leading edge/dowel in proper alignment. Swing the club back slowly until the backswing is complete Here's **Check Point #1:**

THE CLUBSHAFT SHOULD BE ALIGNED PARALLEL WITH THE TARGET LINE. THE LEADING EDGE DOWEL SHOULD BE ANGLED DOWN TOWARD THE TARGET LINE.

Now, move the club very slowly in the Downswing (using the proper body movements we've discussed in previous chapters) to get to the

Check Point #1: Notice that the dowel attached to the bottom of the clubface (the "leading edge") is pointed down at the imaginary target line. The club shaft itself, however, is parallel to the target line and may even be pointing at the target itself, though not necessarily.

... **Stay In The Mind**

beginning of the Forwardswing. You are now ready for **Check Point #2:**

THE CLUB SHAFT SHOULD BE ALIGNED TO POINT TO THE TARGET LINE, ABOUT TWO FEET FORWARD OF THE BALL LOCATION. THE LEADING EDGE/DOWEL (AS SHOWN IN THIS ILLUSTRATION) SHOULD BE ALIGNED IN A DIRECTION THAT SHOULD ALSO POINT TO THE TARGET LINE, ABOUT FIVE FEET BACK FROM WHERE THE BALL IS LOCATED.

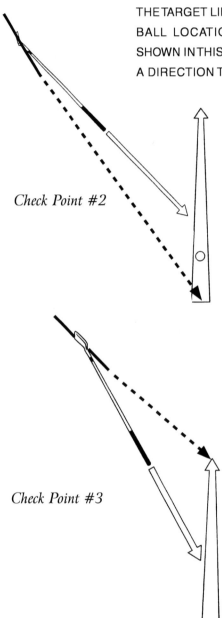

Check Point #2

Check Point #3

From the beginning of the Forwardswing position, move the club and body very slowly through Impact and continue to move past the end of the Forwardswing position into the Up-and-Around movement. Stop when the hands are at hip level and the club shaft and left forearm create a 90-degree angle. Here's **Check Point #3:**

THE CLUB SHAFT SHOULD BE ALIGNED TO POINT TOWARD THE TARGET LINE ABOUT THREE FEET BACK FROM WHERE THE BALL WAS LOCATED BEFORE BEING "HIT." THE LEADING EDGE/DOWEL SHOULD BE ANGLED TO POINT TOWARD THE TARGET LINE, ABOUT FOUR FEET FORWARD OF WHERE THE BALL WAS LOCATED.

You can easily see these three checkpoints reflected in the mirror.
You also may have noticed something very similar about the descriptions of the alignment of the club shaft and

leading edge relative to the target line — namely, they're both pointed somewhere along it at each Check Point.

Check Point #4

Check point #4 is a little different. Continue the Up-and-Around Swing very slowly until you have reached the Kodak Moment. At this point, the swing movement is simply responding to the movements that have preceded it. You achieve your Kodak Moment as the body attempts to balance itself in relation to the momentum you've created during the Forwardswing and the Up-and-Around Swing.

Allow the club to go where it wants to. Its position at the end of the completed swing will vary with the kind of the club used and the shot played.

Check Point #4 is simply the end of the swing. You allow the miracle to happen, maintain your balance and stand tall. Check the mirror to see where you ended up!

There you have it, the four areas to check and the parts of the club to observe in those areas. Go through these check points several times. Get an idea of where you are and where the club is. Your golf game will never be the same — I guarantee it.

WHETHER DRIVER OR WEDGE . . .
ALIGN THE SHAFT AND THE LEADING EDGE!

WHEN SHAFT AND LEADING EDGE ALIGN . . .
EVERY SHOT WILL BE FINE!

... Stay In The Mind

Chapter 10: Impact

The Most Important Part of the Swing

Everything we've learned thus far in the book will be judged, at least on the course, by one criterion and one criterion alone: Impact. This is the only part of the swing that determines ball flight. Your grip, swing movement, ball placement, feet and knee position, posture, swing plane and COB are all means to this end.

This, as they say, is the moment of truth. This is the moment the clubface collides with the ball and sends it on its way.

Let's take a look at a few of our Universals from the Introduction that directly relate to Impact:

6. The golf ball only responds to the club during Impact.
7. IMPACT is the most important part of the golf swing.
9. The ball does not know who you are.

I have noted, on several occasions, that some golfers feel that the ball has let them down, judging by the various names they shout after it as it heads for the woods, bunker or water hazard.

O innocent golf ball! It has no idea what your body is doing during Impact. The ball responds only to the circumstances and conditions created by the club.

I'll state the obvious: The better we are at getting our body into a position that is efficient and requires the least amount of compensation, the better we'll be able to repeat a swing that will return the club to the proper position at Impact. That, my fellow golfers, is consistency. Off the tee . . . middle of the fairway . . . on the green . . . in the cup.

As you've probably figured out by now, I like to find situations and images from everyday life to help

Lessons That Rhyme . . .

golfers picture the parts of the golf swing. This one came to me while on a Christmas shopping trip in downtown Atlanta.

I was going into a large department store in search of a gift for Joyce. The main entrance had a large, revolving door. It was a busy place so you had to have pretty good timing when it was your turn. My timing was slightly off, and my backside was gently nudged as the door came around.

An image flashed before me, and I turned around to watch the door at work. It just kept bumping people into the store like . . . golf balls.

Remember the movie, "Caddy Shack"? Remember Bill Murray's great line, "Be the ball"? OK, picture this: The revolving door is the clubface. You are the ball. The door/clubface comes in at an angle and bumps your backside, pushing you through the door.

"That's Impact!" I exclaimed, causing a few shoppers move a little further away from me.

I suppose that Irish writer would have called this an "epiphany." I call it a great way to visualize a golf club hitting a golf ball.

Clubface at Impact

How often have you heard that "the clubface must be square to the target at Impact?" Well, it's simply not true. That one statement has led many players to leave the clubface open through Impact in a futile attempt to "square it up" with the target.

Impact has three phases: contact, compression and separation. Let's look at each phase and see how it can help us (see illustration on page 42).

Phase 1: Contact. This is when the clubface surface first touches the outer surface of the ball. The clubface is slightly open in relation to the target

Impact has three distinct phases: contact, compression and separation. Though short-lived, Impact is by no means a mere "moment."

... Stay In The Mind

line. Therefore, it is open to the target.

Phase 2: Compression. I promised to keep things simple, but at this point talking a little physics can greatly improve our understanding of what's going on here. Simply stated, the ball is softer that the club; therefore, the ball will be compressed due to the force of the more dense implement, becoming flatter on the side upon which it was struck.

3 PHASES OF IMPACT

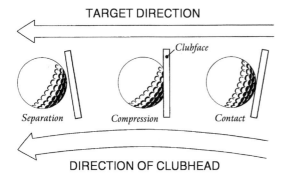

TARGET DIRECTION

Clubface

Separation   Compression   Contact

DIRECTION OF CLUBHEAD

Varying degrees of flatness will occur due to the type, angle and velocity of the clubhead when compression takes place. Immediately following initial Impact, the ball will remain on the clubface for only about five ten-thousands of a second, regardless of the clubhead speed — even with a slow-moving putter. It is still only one-half of a millisecond. (This is from *In Search of the Perfect Golf Swing* by Alastair Cochran and John Stobbs, a great book for those interested in the science of the golf swing.) Research indicates that for an entire 18 holes of golf, the ball is on the clubface for less that one-half second. During the Compression phase, the clubface is continuing to close its angle and will become square to the target.

Phase 3: Separation. This is where the ball and clubface part company. Because of the arc of the clubhead, its face will be slightly closed to the target when this occurs.

Don't think square. Think of the motion during Impact. Think of the clubface moving through the ball, colliding with the ball. Think of the movement

👆 *During Contact, the clubface is slightly open in relation to the target. In the Compression phase, the clubface continues to close its angle and will become square to the target. Because of the clubhead's arc, the clubface will be slightly closed to the target during Separation.*

of the clubface. If you think "square" you'll have a tendency to "guide" the clubface and try to make it meet the ball "squarely." In virtually every instance, you'll be "guiding" the ball . . . *to the far right!*

Body Parts at Impact

Our body and its parts should be graceful and in a powerful, balanced position to create the maximum amount of speed. (Remember Fred and Ginger?)

Here's another mystery exposed: *The Impact position of the body and body parts are not the same as they were at the Address position.*

During Impact there is more weight on the front foot than on the back one due to the lateral movement of the COB (see pages 30-31). Both arms are continuing to extend. The hips are turned only far enough so that the belt buckle is pointed to a spot on the target line about 12 to 14 inches forward of the ball.

Your head has moved to the right of the position it occupied at Address. It has done so in response to the upper spine movement during the Backswing. Your right shoulder is a little lower and nearer to the target line than it was at Address. The left shoulder is just a bit further from the target line, and your right palm is facing the target!

Let's look at the parts.

Feet: The right foot pushes from the inside ball of the foot to assist in creating the lateral movement of the COB. The left foot accepts the weight as it is transferred. It will respond to the additional weight transfer and will roll toward the outer edge as your weight continues to transfer in that direction.

Knees: They respond to the pushing of the right foot and assist by moving in a lateral direction toward the target. Both knees are somewhat flexed

The object of the swing is to allow the clubface to "return" to the ball with the least amount of compensation and the greatest amount of efficiency. The body is not in the same position it was at Address.

... Stay In The Mind

The legs, when moved properly, assist the power-producers — the hips, abdominal muscles, shoulders, arms, wrists and hands. Think of the legs as a "balancing platform."

and have moved a considerable distance from their initial location at Address. The right knee has moved further than the left.

Legs: Both have moved with the COB movement, knee movement, and from the pushing of the right foot and the responsiveness of the left. *The legs are simply a balancing platform.* When moved properly, they assist the power-producers — the hips, abdominal muscles, shoulders, arms, wrists and hands. The legs alone do not produce power; they aid in the creation of power by moving properly and at the appropriate time.

Hips: They resist and rotate. At the proper time, they direct the movement of the abdominal muscles. The abdominal muscles direct the shoulders. The shoulders direct the arms. The hips begin to rotate as the lateral COB motion has started to transfer the weight to the front foot. When the hips rotate with the proper COB movement, they become the first link in a chain reaction, triggering the other body parts to move gracefully and in harmony. The result will produce your most efficient, consistent swing.

Here's a mental cue to help you:

**THINK OF THE CLUBFACE AS A REVOLVING DOOR . . .
DURING IMPACT YOU MUST CLOSE IT TO SCORE!**

CHAPTER 11: Distance
The Long of It

The most beautiful sight in golf is when the ball drops into the hole and you've pared (or done better). No question. But a sight that rivals even a birdie putt is a ball sailing off the tee, right down the center of the fairway, further than the eye can see.

I'll always remember a student of mine who was well into his seventh decade and still shot his age. His ball always landed in the middle and came to rest some 225 yards down the fairway. He could out-putt every one of my other students. The sand was just another surface to him. The gracefulness of his swing reminded me of a cross between the ballet dancer Rudolf Nureyev doing a pirouette and baseball great Hank Aaron hitting a home run.

We all love distance. There is no one secret to it. Virtually every part of the golf swing influences how far you're going to hit the ball. It doesn't matter how tall you are or how much you weigh. It's a matter of how well you swing and how much clubhead speed you can build up (more on this in a moment).

But there's one distance-killer that affects many golfers: tension. *Tension is the direct result of uncertainty and fear.* For the most part, this uncertainty and fear is the result of not understanding the swing, the inability to perform the swing with consistency, or never having the opportunity to be ex-

Tension — the direct result of uncertainty and fear — is to blame for most failed attempts to achieve distance.

... Stay In The Mind

All the knowledge and practice in the world can't help your swing if you're too tense to maintain supple wrists and a natural rhythm. Shake and stretch your arms! Roll you head on your shoulders! Loosen up!

posed to basic fundamentals and/or preferences.

Tension makes us rigid. Our hands, wrists and arms lose their suppleness. We can't sustain a natural rhythm. We become frustrated, and one bad shot follows another.

Tension is created in the mind but it reveals itself in the body. Relief from uncertainty and fear is a matter of gaining confidence through knowledge. But out on the course is not the time to review fundamentals. For temporary relief, we can borrow an old trick actors and singers use just before they go out on stage. Long distance runners do the same thing.

Though its effects are temporary, try shaking and stretching your arms and legs. Roll your head in a circular motion on your shoulders. Then let your body go completely limp. Remember these rhymes:

TO KEEP YOUR BODY TENSION-FREE . . .
SHAKE YOUR ARMS & LEGS BEFORE TAKING THE TEE!

FOR GREATER DISTANCE FROM THE TEE . . .
MAKE SURE YOUR SWING IS TENSION FREE!

Now that you feel reasonably comfortable with the Universals, Absolutes and Essentials of the golf swing (see Introduction for discussion), here are some tips that will add yards to every ball you hit!

Velocity, Lag and COB

The faster the clubhead is traveling during Impact, the more energy you're going to transfer from clubhead to the ball. The more energy transferred, the further the ball will go. Increase velocity and you increase distance. How do we increase velocity? We increase the "lag time."

Lag? No, it is not a Southernism for "leg." Lag time begins when a 90-degree angle between the left arm and the club shaft is achieved, after the Forwardswing begins. Take a look at the illustration below.

The "lag angle" isn't something you "set." It just

The quicker you move your hands from your right thigh to the "Y," with the wrist remaining supple, the longer the "lag angle" will be maintained and the more velocity you will impart during Impact.

happens naturally when you allow your wrists to be supple, keep your arms moving, and maintain the other Absolutes of the golf swing.

Recall the "Y" we make after Impact? The quicker you move your hands from your right thigh to the "Y," with the wrist remaining supple, the longer the "lag angle" will be maintained and the more velocity you will impart during Impact. Here's a rhyme to help:

THE LONGER THE LAG . . .
THE LESS CLUB YOU'LL NEED TO REACH THE FLAG!

Fortunately, we've got two things going for us to help us maintain that lag until the last moment and then to move it with lightning speed from the

... Stay In The Mind

Weight transfer to the left foot cannot occur without the COB moving in the same direction.

right thigh to "Y." They are our old friends COB and gravity (both discussed in chapter 1). When the lateral movement of the COB quits, the hands have to hit the ball. We don't have a choice. Gravity will unhinge the wrists and bring the clubhead down, if we allow the miracle to happen. Moved by the natural motion of our body, the clubface will swing through the ball.

Weight can't be transferred toward the left foot without the COB moving in the same direction. Look at our two golfers here. Proper movement of the COB will transfer your weight to your left foot. This rhyme will help remedy that situation.

NO

YES

On the Swing-A-Way:

KEEP YOUR BUCKLE ON THE BALL . . .
AND WATCH YOUR HANDICAP FALL!

And during the Forwardswing:

THE FASTER THE HANDS MOVE FROM RIGHT THIGH TO "Y" . . .
THE FURTHER AND STRAIGHTER THE SHOTS WILL FLY!

There are other elements of the swing we've covered in previous chapters that also come into play to help you gain those extra 20 yards. But if you'll follow the above advice, you too will be shooting your age when you're in your seventh decade!

Chapter 12: Primary Objective
Get the Ball in the Hole

These final chapters deal with "immediate relief," information you can use right away to improve your game, even before you build a good, consistent swing. I've included this information because I want you to enjoy your game more — *right now*. For instance, if you had a tournament tomorrow, I would suggest you employ "The Dot Game" scoring technique on page 52. It doesn't involve a change in swing, just a change in attitude. As I've often said, there's a time and place for every band-aid. Here are a few to add to your first-aid kit.

Go Forth and Score Well

One of my prize pupils came to beautiful Golf Meadows with a long face after a tournament one day. He had ended up five strokes behind the lead.

"I hit the ball well, Charlie. I just couldn't score," he said as he picked up a bucket of balls and headed out to the practice tee.

"What was the problem?" I asked.

"I'm not sure. I had perfect balance, tempo, rhythm. People kept telling me how beautiful my swing was. I don't know." He took some graceful warm-up swings and started his practice routine.

How can you play well and not score? Is that possible?

You betcha'. Allow me once again to state the

It is possible to play well and swing well — and yet still not score well. Remember, you will be measured by how many shots it takes you to play the course, not how well you played each shot.

... Stay In The Mind

Your game will continue to improve with practice. Don't worry if you find yourself having to compromise your "perfect" swing movement in order to make a certain shot. Score!

obvious: Neither credit nor strokes are taken off the card for your golf knowledge or swing technique. A player is measured only by how many strokes it took him or her to play the course. It's not how, but how many. If, other than having a good time, your objective is to win, you must develop a movement that will give you the best score, given your present ability.

Yes, this is your pro talking. If your goal is to get the lowest possible score on the course, I would rather see you develop a way to do *that* than try to develop the perfect swing movement. You have my permission, within the rules of the game, to score well. I don't care which club you use. I don't care how big your golf bag is. Score well. Your game will continue to improve as you work on your swing on the practice tee and become more proficient. But if you have a game today, I say go forth and score well. Play your own game, not one out of a book. Be innocent. Be confident. Do the best with what you have.

I am reminded of my daughter in junior high. She was trying out for the basketball team (the first time she had ever shown an interest in any organized athletic activity). She was in her early teenage, tripping-over-everything years and came bursting into the kitchen after her first practice. Her face was beaming with excitement. Her energy filled the room.

"Dad, Dad, Dad!" she screamed, practically knocking the screen door off its hinges. "Coach said I only had to work on three things! Isn't that great?" Her smile set fire to everything around her.

I returned her smile. "What three things, hon?"

"Dribbling, passing and shooting!"

She made the team.

Be innocent. I don't care if you just started this wonderful game or have been mashing the ball for fifty years. Score with whatever you've got.

Here are three basic reasons high-handicappers don't score well, and what you can do immediately on the course to improve your game.

Reason #1: *You underclub.* Most golfers think they can hit the ball further than they really can. Pride? Ego? Vanity? I don't care if everybody else *did* use a seven iron. If you think it might take you a six, five or four, go with your instinct, not your ego.

Get on the green. Remember, the number on your scorecard is more important than the number on your club. Score.

Reason #2: *You attempt a shot beyond your skill level.* You have a choice: a 180-yard carry over water, or a lay up shot to your right, which will add a stroke to your game. You have been able to keep your ball airborne for 180 yards, let's see, *three times in your life!* Everyone else in your foursome goes over the water. What is your choice?

Lay up. Make it up on the green. Score.

Reason #3: *You "play the golf swing" rather than "play the game."* That's why my student couldn't score. I make a living helping you swing better. You can "play the golf swing" all you want when you're with me. But when you are out on the course, "play the game." Enjoy. Have fun. *Score!*

Peer pressure on the course is as real as it is anywhere else in the world. Just remember: No matter which club everyone else uses, no matter how aggressive their game strategy, play the game you are most comfortable playing. When it's all said and done, you will have shot your lowest possible score.

USE A SWING AND CLUB YOU CAN CONTROL . . .

AND GET THE BALL TO THE HOLE!

IT'S NOT THE NUMBER ON THE CLUB YOU HIT . . .

IT'S THE NUMBER ON THE CARD YOU GET!

Now, here are two "games" you can play to help you. Both are quite simple, but like so many simple things in life, surprisingly enlightening.

... Stay In The Mind

The Dot Game

We've talked about "swing consistency" and the importance of developing a "repeatable swing motion." The Dot Game underscores this necessity. It enables you to compare the game you could have played (with a more consistent swing) to the game you actually played.

This is an excellent way to get you excited about the talent you *already* possess. The purpose of this game is to see what is possible at your current skill level.

Play your normal game. However, when you attempt a shot that you sincerely believe you have enough skill to accomplish and the ball comes to rest shy of the hole, place a dot on your scorecard. To avoid a dot, you don't have to land on the green — just be even or above the hole. We're only concerned with proper distance here. Take the shot that you honestly feel you can accomplish, and if you miss it, put a dot on the card.

At the end of the game, add up your score, then add up your dots. Divide the total number of dots by two and subtract that number from your score. Here's an example:

										IN	TOT	DOTS	SHOULD SHOOT
Golf Meadows													
11	12	13	14	15	16	17	18						
4	7	6	4	4	8	7	4			¹⁰/₅₀	98	¹⁸/₉	89

Tour total score is 98. Total dots is 18 — divided by 2, that's 9. Subtract 9 from 98. That gives you 89! Just think: You could have broken 90!

The Greenback Game

One of the toughest shots for any player is to get the ball to the cup when the flag stick is on the back of the green. There is always a fear of going over, or "flying," the green. Here is a game that will help you lose that fear. It's fun, and you even get to pick up your ball and move it!

No matter where the flag stick is located, attempt to hit the ball to the back cut of the green without going over the fringe. The distance you stop the ball from the back cut portion of the green is the distance you can bring the ball to the hole.

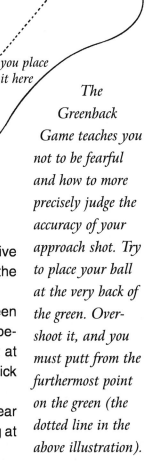

your ball lands here

you place it here

Here's an example. Let's say you stop the ball one foot from the back of the green (see illustration). You get to pick up your ball and place it one foot from the hole. If your ball stops five feet from the back, you place it five feet from the hole.

Now, if you go over the surface of the green and your ball comes to rest on the fringe or beyond, you have to pick up the ball and place it at the furthest point on the green from the flag stick and putt from there.

Believe me, you'll soon learn to hit the ball near but not over. Practice this drill and you'll be firing at the flag stick no matter where it is.

The Greenback Game teaches you not to be fearful and how to more precisely judge the accuracy of your approach shot. Try to place your ball at the very back of the green. Over-shoot it, and you must putt from the furthermost point on the green (the dotted line in the above illustration).

THE PLAYER THAT'S WEAK FROM FEAR . . .
WILL NEVER GET THE BALL NEAR!

Forget pride. Take enough club. Be innocent. Be confident. Use the swing you can control. The number on the score card is the only one that counts.

... Stay In The Mind

Chapter 13: Save the Worms

Cures for the Dismal Duo

We may pray for a nice, high trajectory, but our ball sometimes sails no higher than the top of the grass. The well-named "worm burner" defeats us before we leave the tee box. This is one of the most frustrating results of a poor golf swing.

The other villain is the shocking slice. I say "shocking" because we usually go into a mild state of shock as we watch the ball start left of the target line then rapidly curve to the right, cross the target line and head for OB (the trees, a lake, house, an adjoining fairway, another golfer).

What's worse than a worm-burner or slice? Right! A sliced worm-burner. It even sounds gristly. Let's take these problems in order — *and cure them!*

Topping the Ball

There's nothing more frustrating than topping the ball and hitting a "worm-burner." Luckily, the problem is easily corrected.

Your foursome cries "worm burner" and you sulk down to the long grass just beyond the front tees for your second shot.

When you attempt to eradicate all life forms at ground level, it's called "topping the ball." For a variety of reasons, we hit the top of the ball, causing the ball to spin forward. To get airborne — and save the worms for our next fishing trip — the ball must have some degree of back spin. So far, we've rhymed the proper way in which the clubface must collide with the ball during Impact, as well as the appropriate body and swing motions necessary to get the clubface were it needs to be. Now it's time to pen a few rhymes to cure the topped shot. They will remind you what to do and what not to do as you prepare to swing.

RIGHT ELBOW HIGH . . . WATCH THE BALL FLY!

We've been told, time and again, to keep the right elbow jammed into our right side to avoid a "flying right elbow." Well, no good player really does this. If we keep the right elbow at our side during the Backswing, we're going to attempt to hit the ball during the Forwardswing when the clubhead is already on its way up. It's just physically impossible to hit it any other way. If the clubhead is moving up when it meets the ball, the ball will either have no spin or you'll give it a forward spin, driving it to the ground. Allow the right elbow to move naturally (see illustration) away from the body — though never higher than the right shoulder — and there will be much more air between your ball and the fairway!

Don't keep your right elbow jammed into your right side during the swing. If you do, you cannot move properly during the Down-swing and will instead top the ball in the For-ward-swing, when the club face is on its way up.

A CHICKEN WING IS AN UGLY SIGHT . . .
AND ITS BOUND TO PRODUCE AN UGLY BALL FLIGHT!

... Stay In The Mind

The left elbow "chicken wing" is to be avoided at all costs. It occurs when you shove your right elbow into your side or when the COB stops moving, leaving the left arm no choice but to bend at the elbow.

Now let's look at this left elbow. I'm sure chicken wings are very beautiful to other chickens. But in the golf swing, they're plain ugly. When we shove our right elbow into our side, there is nowhere for it to continue to swing. So the left arm will attempt to pull the club forward to hit the ball. Yes, you guessed it: a chicken wing.

Instead of a chicken wing, let nature take her course. Make sure your arms are soft during Impact, in the Forwardswing, and the Up-and-Around Swing. Allow the COB to continue to move forward. As a result, the left forearm will fold toward the body as the right forearm continues to remain extended and will cross on the left.

Bass fishermen (and fisherwomen) know the feeling. When you remove the hook from a bass' mouth after pulling the bottom lip downward, the fish goes limp. That's just how I want your arms to feel during the entire swing!

We've now learned we will hit the ball with our hands wherever we stop our COB (not good). Yet we've also read in other books or have been told around the course that the first motion in the Swing-A-Way, the first part of our Backswing, is to rotate our hips. No successful professional does that! If we intentionally rotate our hips in the Swing-A-Way we'll be tempted to move our COB and end up with most of our weight on the right foot. So we must then rotate our hips enough to get back to the ball, but by then it's too late. This swing sequence causes us to hit the ball with our weight — and our belt buckle — in the wrong spot. Nature demands we hit with our hands when the belt buckle quits, but we don't want to hit with our hands. This not only causes a topped ball, but it guarantees a slice. Remember, there are very few things worse than a sliced worm-burner.

Lessons That Rhyme ...

To correct this problem, just remember to continue the movement of the belt buckle — lateral and around at the same time. This will promote a *continuous lateral movement* of the COB and give you a completed swing rather than one that stopped before we were really finished.

WHEN THE BELT BUCKLE QUITS (MOVING PROPERLY)...
THE HANDS HAVE TO HIT!

The Slice

Do you often find yourself walking down the right side of the fairway, jabbing your club into the bushes? Do you map your ball's path by looking up at tree trunks on the right for recently scared bark or broken limbs?

The slice is the result of you putting clockwise side-spin on the ball during Impact, causing it to curve right. Typically, to produce a slice, your forward club path direction must be traveling quite a bit left of the target, with the clubface aligned to the right of the club path direction.

The slice has a vast array of causes, from improper Essentials (grip, stance, posture), to improper swing movements. *However, the #1 body movement that causes the slice is the improper movement of the COB in the Downswing!* By moving your COB in any direction except in a forward, lateral path, your body parts are forced out of position during the swing. This causes you to have to make an awkward movement simply to make contact with the ball without falling down.

Luckily, there's an easy cure. At first you may pull a few to the left (ever been on the left before?), but to a slicer that's heaven. Try the following:

The slice may be the effect of any number of causes — from improper Essentials (grip, stance, posture), to improper swing movements. But the #1 body movement that causes the slice is the improper movement of the COB in the Downswing.

... Stay In The Mind

The right forearm crosses over the left (chapter 3). The earlier the crossover, the quicker the club face will close.

1. Hold handle more in the fingers than the palm (chapter 2).

2. Make sure your arms are soft (chapter 3).

3. Check for proper shoulder alignment and good posture (chapter 5).

4. Keep your right knee in the same location during the Backswing (chapter 8).

5. As you swing with your soft arms, allow your right forearm to cross over your left forearm (chapter 3). The earlier this crossover happens, the less the ball will travel to the right.

Beside the photograph of your spouse, children or other loved one(s) in your wallet, place a small but easily read copy of this rhyme:

LET THE FOREARMS CROSS . . .
AND SHOW THE BALL WHO'S BOSS.

Goodbye slice. *Hello distance!*

Chapter 14: Drilling for Par

How Quickly Do You Want to Improve?

Notwithstanding those at the dentist's office, I really like drills. Drills help us *feel* correct movements . . . over and over again. A friend of mine told me a long time ago, "If a picture is worth a thousand words, a feeling is worth a million!"

Good drills create good habits, and drills can be done just about anywhere. Like my dentist says, "This won't hurt a bit." And he's right. He performs the procedure correctly.

Many of my students ask, "How often should I practice my drills, Charlie?"

My answer is always the same: "How quickly do you want to improve?" I know there are many more important things out there than golf. You've got a busy, demanding life. But your improvement will be based upon your dedication and desire to play well, and that ultimately will involve practice.

This lesson came home to me (quite literally) several years ago. When my youngest daughter was all of four years old, she was selected to play the part of Gretel in a high school production of "The Sound of Music." She wanted to do well. She practiced her lines and songs night and day. She practiced her movements. She watched the movie until even I knew all the words! A few nights before opening, Joyce and I went in to check on her to discover that she was going over her lines and songs.

We've said it before, but it's worth saying again: There are no quick-fix "secrets" to the perfect golf game. Your improvement will be based entirely upon your dedication and desire to play well, and that ultimately will involve practice. Here are three practice drills that can dramatically improve your swing.

. . . Stay In The Mind

What made it so unusual was that she was sound asleep at the time!

She did a sensational job in all the performances.

How often should you practice drills?

How strong is your desire?

The Stork Drill

The Stork Drill enables you to experience most of your weight on the left foot when hitting the ball.

One of my favorites is the "Stork Drill." This one drill will help you create the proper movements in *eleven* areas of the golf swing.

The Stork Drill allows you to "feel" what it is like to have most of your weight on the left foot when hitting the golf ball. Many golfers have never experienced this sensation because they've never understood how to transfer their weight during the

swing. I quickly discovered, however, that while I created the Stork Drill for this specific purpose, its usefulness was far more encompassing.

First, let's get into the correct position so we can perform the drill. By following the illustrations, you'll soon discover what makes this drill so useful.

1. Assume the correct Address position with a five iron in hand as though you were going to hit a normal shot.

2. Elevate your right foot approximately twelve inches off the ground and rest the inside ball of your right foot on something that will give you balance. There should be as little weight as possible on your right foot and about 99% of it on your left.

Twelve inches, by the way, is optimum. I use a very large sponge for my students. The softness

Follow these steps and the illustrations below to perform The Stork Drill. As you'll see, it will help you improve your swing motion and allow you to "feel" what it's like to hit the ball with most of your weight on your left foot.

... Stay In The Mind

The Stork Drill enables you to experience your individual swing movement without having to focus all of your attention on the proper transfer of your COB — the most difficult component of the swing. By elevating your right foot, your COB remains relatively station-ary, enabling you to concentrate on other facets of the swing discussed in the chapter.

"shows" and allows them to "feel" how much weight is on the right foot. (Note: you can use just about anything that's twelve inches high, from an upside-down ball basket to your golf bag laying on the ground.)

Make sure your right foot is back far enough from the target line to let you swing your arms and hands straight back without hitting your right knee.

3. Balance yourself by putting more weight on the ball of the left foot, with almost no weight on the heel. You should sense the heel being near the ground but with very little weight on it. The left knee should have some flex. The flex is for balance and to relieve any stiffness in the left leg.

4. Stand as tall as possible while balancing yourself. Allow your arms to simply hang down in a very relaxed manner. The ball should be as near to you as possible. Remember what the great Mr. Gene Sarazen said: "You cannot stand too close to the ball while hitting it."

Note: In the remaining steps, you may have to experiment with placing the ball in a few locations before your clubface is able to make solid contact.

5. Swing the club back with your arms, allow-ing your shoulders to respond in a "winding up" motion. Let your wrists hinge naturally until you "feel" that you have completed the Backswing movement. Always check your balance!

6. After you complete the Backswing move-ment, the Downswing begins. Allow gravity to be a great part of the gradual acceleration of the arm movement with supple wrists. When you perform the Stork Drill, there will be very little movement of The lower body because most of the weight was already on the left foot to begin with. However, there will be some movement due to the swinging of the arms and momentum of the upper body.

Lessons That Rhyme ...

7. After you complete the Downswing movement and you begin the Forwardswing, the right elbow begins to unfold, extending the right arm. The left arm will continue to be extended throughout the entire Forwardswing movement. You should feel no tension in either arm as they continue to swing toward Impact.

8. Your left arm remains extended while your right arm continues to straighten during Impact until the end of the Forwardswing movement. This is the only time in the golf swing that both arms are fully extended. This, ladies and gentlemen, is the "Y."

9. After Impact, the body will continue to remain in balance. The arms continue to swing with the elbows folding naturally in response to the club swing. Because of the position of your right foot, however, your Forwardswing will be somewhat restricted, and you won't be able to achieve a normal full finish.

When you are performing this drill correctly, you will feel the same body movements and sensations that you would feel during the full swing. All good golfers, when starting from the Address position, will achieve the same Impact position as though they were standing on a sponge, with more weight on their left foot than their right.

One of my new students just couldn't get off his right foot. He tried until he was, quite literally, blue in the face. So I got him in the Address position and told him to lift his right foot.

I got down on all fours and placed my hands on the turf, palms up, under his nice, new (sharp) spikes. I told him to hit the ball.

Not wanting to hurt his pro, he hit the ball with most of his weight on his left foot for the first time in his life! My hands remained whole, and he was de-

Although your Forwardswing will be somewhat restricted and you won't be able to achieve a normal full finish, when you perform the drill correctly, you will nevertheless feel the same body movements and sensations that you would feel during the full swing.

... Stay In The Mind

lighted with his shot.

But the Stork Drill will help you to do more than simply keep your weight off your right foot. Let's look at the 11 areas of the swing that the drill will improve.

BENEFITS OF THE STORK DRILL

1. It ensures that most of our weight is on the left foot during Impact.

2. It promotes the correct swinging direction of the arms and club during the Swing-A-Way.

3. It tells you immediately if your hands are doing anything except holding onto the handle as the arms swing. It promotes the feeling that you don't have to do anything with your hands other than hold on and let gravity be your friend.

4. It promotes suppleness in the wrists throughout the entire swing movement.

5. It creates the feeling of balance as the arms swing and the body responds to that movement.

6. It allows you to feel your head responding to the upper spine relocation as the correct shoulder movement is made during the "wind-up" segment of the Backswing.

7. It promotes the proper folding of the right elbow, as well as the extended condition of the left arm, during the Backswing movement.

8. It promotes the proper position of your head during Impact.

9. It eliminates the tendency to squat during any part of the swinging motion.

10. It promotes the right forearm's crossing over the left as the arms are swinging during the Forwardswing and beyond.

11. It promotes the proper location of the hands. During Impact, your hands should be forward of the belt buckle but not outside the left thigh.

Lessons That Rhyme ...

The Split Hand Drill

Use a five iron. The Split Hand drill gives the golfer the proper feeling of forearm movement during the Forwardswing. To perform this drill:

1. Assume your proper grip and stance. Raise the shaft to a horizontal location *(1.)* in front of you.

2. Move your right hand down the handle until the thumb and first finger touch the shaft, keeping the left hand in its original location. Hold the handle, as normal, in your right hand. That will position the right hand about three inches down from the left.

(2.)

3. Keep the shaft horizontal while swinging your arms back and swinging them through. During the

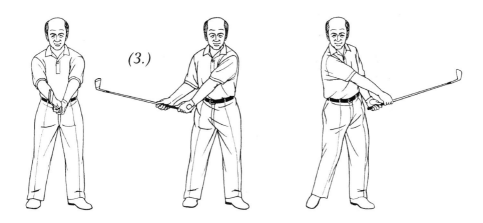

(3.)

right forearm cross over your left. As your arms extend and the right forearm crosses over the left, continue to maintain that extended arm condition as the arms are fully crossed.

Continue the swinging motion, allowing the forearms to cross while gradually tilting forward with

... Stay In The Mind

your upper spine until you reach your normal Address position. You should not be able to brush the grass with the leading edge of the club. If you can, you've titled too far forward and you're out of position.

On the golf course, do this drill two or three times in the Address position before you hit the ball. Place your hands in their normal location. Then set up, and *hit the ball.*

The PVC Drill: "Positive Visual Concepts"

The PVC Drill was designed to prevent "dipping" of the left shoulder during the swing movement. Like The Stork Drill, however, it promotes efficient, repeatable movements in other areas as well.

This drill was inspired by another true-life lesson on the course. One of my students kept moving his left shoulder down during his Backswing movement, throwing his COB and upper spine out of position

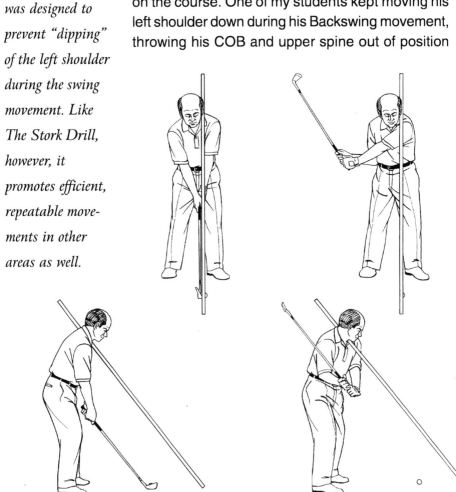

(and creating many other problems as well). I had to do something, so I ran up to the green, yanked the flag stick out of the hole and returned to my student with it. I placed the flag stick on his left shoulder, near his neck, and asked him to assume the Address position while balancing the stick.

Next, I asked him to swing his hands back to just past hip level and stop, not allowing the stick to roll off his shoulder. He did . . . and no more left-shoulder dipping occurred. He was cured.

Since golf courses frown on you "borrowing" their flag sticks, here's what I want you to do.

Go down to your local hardware store, unless you still have the PVC sections left over from

Balance the PVC on your left shoulder but don't attempt to hold it there; incline your spine and it will balance on its own. When it does, you've inclined your spine correctly — and assumed the correct Address position!

. . . Stay In The Mind

The object of The PVC Drill is to keep the stick from moving as you perform an abbreviated swing. This drill forces you to move only the necessary parts of your body that will help you to develop a consistent swing unencumbered by any extraneous movements.

chapter 9, and buy a ten-foot-long, one-inch-diameter, schedule 40, PVC pipe with one end flared. (You'll also need to buy a collar for the pipe if you don't get the flared end).

Note: If you tell the clerk you want a Positive Visual Concepts training aid, you may not get much of a response (unless the clerk happens to be a student at beautiful Golf Meadows). Just pretend you're going to repair the leak in the basement your spouse has been after you to do for five years.

Depending on your ability, either you or the clerk must cut the PVC into two sections, four feet long. (Most stores only sell PVC in ten-foot sections. With the two feet left over, you might be able to repair that leak!)

A flag stick is seven feet long. Your new "Positive Visual Concepts" training aid will be, when you join the two pieces together with the collar, eight feet long. (You cut the section in half so the pieces could fit on your golf bag.)

Here's the drill (refer to illustrations on pages 66-67). Tee up a ball and assume your normal posture at Address. Rest one end of the PVC on the ground, about two feet out from the ball. The distance will vary according to your height. (Remember, you're using your 5 iron for this drill, and the ball is on a tee.)

Balance the PVC on your left shoulder, just about where your neck and shoulder meet. Some of the PVC will extend past your shoulder. Lower your right shoulder and elevate your left to make sure the PVC is balanced there. Don't attempt to hold the PVC with your left shoulder. Incline your spine and it will balance there. When you've got the PVC balanced, you've inclined your spine correctly. You have also assumed the correct Address position! The idea is to keep the PVC from moving as you perform an abbreviated swing.

Now take an abbreviated swing like the figure in the illustrations. In the Swing-A-Way, your hands should go no higher than your hip. But let the wrists hinge to allow the club shaft and left arm to form a 90-degree angle when you reach hip level.

Now swing, hit the ball, and continue past the Forwardswing until the hands reach about hip level during the Up-and-Around Swing. The left forearm and club shaft should form a 90-degree angle.

What happens? The PVC shouldn't move. Hit the ball only about fifty yards during this drill. Try to take advantage of the instantaneous feedback the exercise provides:

BENEFITS OF THE PVC DRILL

1. It keeps you from moving your COB in the Backswing.

2. It promotes the COB to initiate the Downswing and continue moving properly.

3. It prevents you from coming "over the top" in the Downswing (if you do, you'll hit the stick and the PVC will drop off your left shoulder).

4. It takes your hands out of the swing.

5. It helps you create the "Y."

6. It mandates a proper incline of the spine.

7. Your head can't move ahead of the ball.

8. It promotes the crossing of the forearms.

9. The PVC creates a visual plane and helps keep you on *your* plane, as discussed in chapter 7.

Preform the PVC Drill often. In no time, your visions of a great golf shot will not be just a pipe dream!

Like The Stork Drill, the benefits of The PVC Drill are manifold. This is because the golf swing itself, while theoretically composed of many separate movements, is actually only one, complex, graceful motion.

... Stay In The Mind

Final Thoughts

It is my sincerest wish that *Lessons That Rhyme* will give the new player a better understanding of the golf swing, and the veteran player an enjoyable new way of approaching his or her game.

You will always have the challenge of a certain shot, but now you'll know what to do with it. You'll also miss a few now and then, but you'll know why and how to make the correction. Remember from chapter 6: *Nine words plus one phrase equals a "perfect 10."*

If I have made the golf swing easier for you to understand and perform, I have achieved my goal. I greatly appreciate the time we've spent together. Thank you.

Charlie Sorrell, PGA MASTER PROFESSIONAL
Golf Meadows

If you would like to add your rhyme to our collection at Golf Meadows, drop us a note, fax or e-mail us at:

GOLF MEADOWS
1940 FLIPPEN ROAD
STOCKBRIDGE, GA 30281
(FAX) 1-770-957-9554
(E-MAIL) GOLFMEADOW@AOL.COM

Appendix A

To Tee or Not to Tee

The Universals of the Golf Swing

(reprinted from pages xv - xx)

The Universals

Every sport has its "Universals." To make a turn, a snow skier must transfer his or her weight to the right ski or the left. If a pitcher wants to throw a strike in baseball, he or she must manipulate the ball to somehow enter the strike zone.

The following are what I consider the "Universals" for the game of golf. I won't go into detail here, but you'll see them resurface again and again throughout the book. Many may seem obvious, but the human mind is tricky. What looks logical on paper often takes on a whole new meaning when you get to the first tee.

Universal #1: The ball is struck by a player using hand-eye coordination and motor skills.

No matter what kind of club or ball you use, no matter what you paid for your golf bag, no matter how much the greens fees were . . . you, and you alone, are what will make the ball soar. And as difficult as it may seem, hitting a golf ball correctly is actually much less complicated than driving a car and takes about as much physical and mental talent as riding a bike. Ever done either one of those?

. . . Stay In The Mind

I can't help you with hand-eye coordination — your "motor skills," as the medical people call them. You've already developed these. Some of us obviously have better ones than others. However, by learning proper body and club positions and movements, your motor skills will be strengthened as you learn to swing the club in a more efficient manner.

Universal #2: Ball-flight patterns and their causes must be understood.

This takes a little experience in hitting golf balls. Let's get back to the car. If you suddenly hear a pop, see rubber flying in your rearview mirror, and the car starts veering to the left, you can be pretty sure you've blown your left front tire.

The same is true in golf. Illustrated below are the nine horizontal ball-flight patterns you'll see. These patterns are the direct result of conditions created during Impact by:

♦ Club path direction
♦ Clubface position in relation to the club path
♦ Angle of approach
♦ Impact location of ball on the clubface
♦ Clubhead speed upon Impact

I know this sounds like a great deal to consider and understand, but we'll be returning to these characteristics throughout the book. We might as well take fifteen minutes to learn them now.

HORIZONTAL BALL FLIGHT PATTERNS

1. Straight —The ball starts straight on the target line and does not curve as the ball travels forward.

2. Push —The ball starts to the right of the target line and remains in a straight direction.

3. Push Fade — The ball starts to the right of the target line, then continues to curve to the right of the target line.

4. Draw — The ball starts to the right of the target line, then curves gently back toward the target line but does not cross it.

5. Pull — The ball starts to the left of the target line and continues in a straight direction.

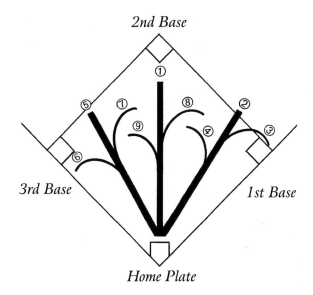

2nd Base

3rd Base

1st Base

Home Plate

6. Pull Hook — The ball starts to the left of the target line and curves abruptly further left, away from the target line.

7. Slice — The ball starts to the left of the target line, then curves abruptly toward the right and crosses the target line.

8. Tail-Away Slice — The ball starts on the target line then, after regaining roundness, curves right.

9. Tail-Away Hook — The ball starts on the target line, then, after regaining roundness, curves left.

Universal #3: A good golf swing is any movement you can repeat, has rhythm, balance and produces the desired shot . . . with minimum

... Stay In The Mind

compensation.

That last part is critical. We all compensate. Some folks say Napoleon tried to conquer the world to compensate for the fact he was short. (My personal opinion is that he should have spent more time on the golf course. Ever notice how many of the best Tour players, with some notable exceptions, aren't all very tall?)

If you jam your toe on a chair while going for that first cup of coffee in a dark kitchen, you favor the foot with the jammed toe as you make your way — more carefully — to the coffee pot. You compensate.

Maybe your wrists aren't quite as flexible as they used to be. You have to make some sort of compensation in your golf swing. You can't perform the perfect golf swing (this is true of Tour players as well as weekend golfers) so you learn to adjust. We must compensate for our uniqueness; we simply want to keep the compensation to a minimum.

Universal #4: Hands determine the clubface position.

That's simple enough. If some people tried to hold a glass of iced tea the way they try to hold a golf club, they'd spill tea all over themselves every time they tried to take a drink. The position of your hands determines whether or not you'll get the tea out of the glass and into your mouth. Think about it.

Universal #5: Shoulder alignment upon Impact (and the use of hands and body parts to get there) influence forward club-path direction.

Take baseball again. You're a righthander and want to hit it to right field. You align your shoulders in that direction. Simple?

Universal #6: The golf ball only responds to the club during Impact.

You can do the Carolina "shag" before you hit the ball and pray to your Creator in the Backswing all you want. The ball will simply sit there, awaiting instructions from your clubface. Which leads me to:

Universal #7: IMPACT is the most important part of the golf swing. See chapter 10.

Universal #8: Your swing motion will be unique.

Look at Arnold Palmer. Chi Chi Rodriguez. Look at Greg Norman. Look at yourself. Your body, your ability, your experience are different than everyone else's. We are individuals. How we get there is where the fun begins.

Universal #9: The ball does not know who you are.

The golf ball may be the most democratic, politically correct item on the face of the earth. It doesn't care if you are male or female. It does not care about your religion, race, color, sex or creed. It doesn't care what you do for a living. It doesn't know which tee you're hitting from. *Attention ladies!* The golf ball will afford you the same courtesy (or disdain) it affords your husband, son, brother or significant other. The golf ball is equality in its purest form.

These are the "Universals." Put a copy in your office, kitchen or garage. I'd tell you to put it in your car, but I don't want to be responsible for accidents. I know golfers.

... Stay In The Mind

Appendix B
The Rhyme List

THE PLAYER WHO SWINGS AND FALLS BACK . . .
WILL NEVER GET THE BALL ON TRACK!

WHEN YOU'RE BALANCED THROUGHOUT THE SWING . . .
A REPEATABLE MOTION IS A SURE THING!

IF YOU DON'T WANT THE COB TO MOVE AT ALL . . .
POINT YOUR RIGHT FOOT AT OR AHEAD OF THE BALL!

SEE THE DOT . . . AND IMPROVE YOUR SHOT!

IF YOU DON'T SEE THAT SPLIT . . .
THE RIGHT HAND DOESN'T FIT!

HIT THE BALL WITH YOUR HANDS . . .
AND YOU'LL NEVER KNOW WHERE IT LANDS!

HOLD THE HANDLE AS YOU SWING . . .
LET GRAVITY DO EVERYTHING!

WRISTS THAT ARE SUPPLE . . .
KEEP YOU OUT OF TROUBLE!

WRISTS THAT ARE TIGHT . . . DESTROY BALL FLIGHT!

Lessons That Rhyme . . .

WRISTS THAT ARE LIMBER . . .
KEEP YOU OUT OF THE TIMBER!

THE SOFTER YOUR ARMS & SHOULDERS CAN BE . . .
THE GREATER YOUR CLUBHEAD'S VELOCITY!

LET THE FOREARMS CROSS . . .
SHOW THE BALL WHO'S BOSS!

THE MORE KNUCKLES YOU SEE . . .
THE FURTHER BACK THE BALL MUST BE!

THE QUICKER YOUR WEIGHT TRANSFER ON THE TEE . . .
THE FURTHER FORWARD YOUR BALL MUST BE!

THE HIGHER YOUR TEE . . .
THE FURTHER FORWARD YOUR BALL MUST BE!

INCLINE YOUR SPINE . . .
AND YOUR SHOT WILL BE FINE!

IF YOUR CAUGHT SQUATTIN' . . .
YOUR SHOT WILL BE ROTTEN!

POINT YOUR CHEST MORE OUT THAN DOWN . . .
THIS POSITION WILL ELIMINATE A FROWN!

ALL GOOD PLAYERS, AT ADDRESS . . .
HANG THEIR ARMS BESIDE THEIR CHEST!

MOVE ALL PARTS IN HARMONY . . .
AND THE CLOSER TO PAR YOU'LL BE!

HANDS HOLD — ARMS SWING — WRISTS HINGE —
ELBOWS FOLD & EXTEND . . .

. . . Stay In The Mind

NINE WORDS AND ONE PHRASE MAKE YOUR SWING A
"PERFECT 10!"

THINK ONE PLANE . . .
AND THE GREEN'S YOUR DOMAIN!

IF YOU'RE NOT ON PLANE . . .
THEY'LL NEVER KNOW YOUR NAME!

BE LIGHT ON YOUR FEET . . .
AND YOUR SWING WILL REPEAT!

THE FLATTER THE FEET . . . THE GREATER THE DEFEAT!

IF YOUR RIGHT KNEE MOVES . . . YOU'RE SURE TO LOSE!

KEEP THE RIGHT KNEE ON THE SPOT . . .
IMPROVE YOUR SWING A LOT!

WHETHER DRIVER OR WEDGE . . .
ALIGN THE SHAFT AND THE LEADING EDGE!

WHEN SHAFT AND LEADING EDGE ALIGN . . .
EVERY SHOT WILL BE FINE!

THINK OF THE CLUBFACE AS A REVOLVING DOOR . . .
DURING IMPACT YOU MUST CLOSE IT TO SCORE!

TO KEEP YOUR BODY TENSION FREE . . .
SHAKE YOUR ARMS AND LEGS BEFORE YOU TAKE THE TEE!

FOR GREATER DISTANCE FROM THE TEE . . .
MAKE SURE YOUR SWING IS TENSION FREE!

THE LONGER THE LAG . . .
THE LESS CLUB YOU'LL NEED TO REACH THE FLAG!

Lessons That Rhyme . . .

KEEP YOUR BUCKLE ON THE BALL . . .
AND WATCH YOUR HANDICAP FALL!

THE FASTER YOUR HANDS MOVE FROM RT. THIGH TO "Y" . . .
THE FURTHER & STRAIGHTER THE SHOTS WILL FLY!

USE A SWING AND CLUB YOU CAN CONTROL . . .
AND GET THE BALL TO THE HOLE!

THE PLAYER WHO IS WEAK FROM FEAR . . .
WILL NEVER GET THE BALL NEAR!

RIGHT ELBOW HIGH . . . WATCH THE BALL FLY!

WHEN THE BELT BUCKLE QUITS (MOVING PROPERLY) . . .
THE HANDS HAVE TO HIT!

About the Authors & Illustrator

Charlie Sorrell, PGA Master Professional

In 1990 Charlie Sorrell was named National Teacher of the Year by the Professional Golfers Association of America. One of *Golf Magazine's* "Top 100 Teachers in America," Sorrell was also selected by the Georgia PGA as that section's Teacher of the Year and Golf Professional of the Year. He has served as the section's president, was co-editor of the *PGA Teaching Journal,* and was an instructor at National PGA schools. He holds three course records, is a former PGA Tour player, and is a regular contributor to several publications, including the *Atlanta Journal-Constitution.*

His ability to relate the golf swing in its simplest terms, using humor and rhymes, has made him highly popular presenter at corporate outings throughout the United States. Sorrell and his wife Joyce make their home at Golf Meadows, a 22-acre private golf-teaching facility just south of Atlanta, Georgia. Conceived of by Sorrell and his wife Joyce, the indoor/outdoor, state-of-the-art center offers instruction to all levels of players from the beginner to the Touring Professional. All lessons are given by Sorrell and are available through advanced reservation only.

Paul deVere

A syndicated golf humor columnist, free-lance journalist and member of the Golf Writers Association of America, deVere has written several golf instruction books, as well as produced numerous video and audio tapes. He is the author of the humorous best-seller, *I GOLF, THEREFORE I AM (frustrated & humble . . . but hopeful),* published by Saron Press, Ltd., 1996. He and his family live on Hilton Head Island, South Carolina.

Shuichi Kuga, Illustrator

Shuichi Kuga's work as a golf artist and sports illustrator is frequently seen in a number of publications worldwide, including *Golf Digest Japan.* He and his wife Sonoko Funakoshi-Kuga, a producer for The Golf Channel, live in Orlando, Florida.